GUIDE FOR
USHERS, GREETERS, AND
MINISTERS OF HOSPITALITY

SECOND EDITION

Karie Ferrell

Corinna Laughlin

Paul Turner

Thomas P. Welch

Nihil Obstat
Rev. Mr. Daniel G. Welter, JD
Chancellor
Archdiocese of Chicago
August 31, 2020

Imprimatur
Most Rev. Ronald A. Hicks
Vicar General
Archdiocese of Chicago
August 31, 2020

The *Nihil Obstat* and *Imprimatur* are declarations that the material is free from doctrinal or moral error, and thus is granted permission to publish in accordance with c. 827. No legal responsibility is assumed by the grant of this permission. No implication is contained herein that those who have granted the *Nihil Obstat* and *Imprimatur* agree with the content, opinions, or statements expressed.

This book was edited by Lorie Simmons. Víctor R. Pérez was the production editor, Anna Manhart was the designer, and Kari Nicholls was the production artist.

29 28 27 26 25   2 3 4 5 6

Printed in the United States of America

Library of Congress Control Number: 2020946511

ISBN: 978-1-61671-591-5

ELUG2

Contents

❦

Preface

*When I entered your house, you did not give me water for my feet,
but she has bathed them with her tears and wiped them with her hair.
You did not give me a kiss, but she has not ceased kissing my feet
since the time I entered. You did not anoint my head with oil, but she
anointed my feet with ointment. So I tell you, her many sins have
been forgiven; hence, she has shown great love.*

—Luke 7:44b–47a

When Jesus appeared at Simon's house for dinner, he had some reasonable expectations. Well, wouldn't you? When you are a guest, someone should welcome you. Someone should be watching out the window for you, ready to open wide the door when you draw near, help you with whatever you're carrying, and shake your hand or give you a hug. Someone should show you the way inside the house, take your coat, let you look around a bit, and help you select a comfortable chair. Someone should offer you a beverage, make sure you know where the restroom is, and start up a friendly conversation.

You have some responsibilities too. You might bring flowers, put a smile on your face, and wipe your feet on the doormat. Upon entering the house, you say how lovely it looks and how good the food smells. You join in the conversation and relax with your host.

Jesus expected nothing more than any other guest would. He expected water to wash his dusty feet, a kindly kiss of welcome, and a little perfume to spice up the visit. Anyone should have done this. Most people did.

But Simon didn't. To make matters worse, Simon was a Pharisee. He may have been an expert in God's law, but he was failing at simple human courtesy.

As St. Luke tells this story (7:36–50), he identifies Simon as a Pharisee to show that his *faux pas* is also a religious scandal. In addition, the title distinguishes this Simon from other Simons in the New Testament. This is not Simon, son of John, the apostle whom Jesus calls "Peter."[1] Nor is it Simon the Zealot, another of the apostles.[2] Judas Iscariot's father's name was Simon.[3] It wasn't him. This isn't Simon, the relative of Jesus.[4] Nor is it Simon the leper, although his story is very similar to this one.[5] It's not Simon of Cyrene, who

---

1. For example, in Matthew 4:18.
2. For example, in Luke 6:15.
3. John 6:71 and 13:26.
4. John 6:71 and 13:26.
5. Matthew 26:6 and Mark 14:3.

would help Jesus carry the cross up Calvary.[6] Nor is it the crooked ex-magician whose desire to buy spiritual power from the apostles gave us the word *simony*,[7] nor Simon the tanner, who must have confused the neighbors when he hosted Simon Peter.[8] It was hard to keep these Simons straight, even in Jesus' day. So Luke calls him Simon the Pharisee. The only New Testament Pharisee named Simon is in this story,[9] and he doesn't make a good impression.

Someone else, though, does. An unnamed woman walks in from the city streets. She is identified only as "a sinful woman," and although we'd like to know her name, Luke may have thought it a courtesy to extend to her this bit of privacy. Some traditions have identified her as Mary Magdalene, and her sin as prostitution, but there's no reason to draw either conclusion. All we know is that her sin was public enough for Simon to call her a certain "sort of woman," and to be repulsed when she touched Jesus. How Simon knew she was a sinner and why she seemed at home in his house are also beyond our speculation.

Jesus, however, isn't fooled into thinking the woman is the only sinner at the table. He tells a parable about two forgiven debtors, and he gets Simon to admit that the one released from the larger debt was the one who loved more. Simon applied the parable correctly: He was like the one with the smaller debt. He could feel relieved that in Jesus' eyes, the woman's debt was greater because her sins were greater than Simon's. But Simon must have been surprised to think that her love was also greater than his.

Jesus had evidence. "When I entered your house, you did not give me water for my feet, but she has bathed them with her tears and wiped them with her hair. You did not give me a kiss, but she has not ceased kissing my feet since the time I entered. You did not anoint my head with oil, but she anointed my feet with ointment."[10] He does not deny that whatever gave this woman her reputation was sinful, but he won't let Simon off the hook.

Hospitality meant something to Jesus. It was more than common custom. Hospitality showed respect for the visitor. It demonstrated the humility of the host. It avoided the temptation to sneer at the less fortunate or the less moral.

In concrete terms, being hospitable means learning people's names and professions, taking care of their simplest needs, and thinking well of them, no matter what their reputation. It assumes that after inviting them in, you know what to do when the guest actually enters. It means being aware of your own tendencies to sin, and make mistakes, so that you do not consider yourself above your guest. You can thus receive every visitor as you would receive Christ.

—Paul Turner

---

6. Matthew 27:32.
7. Acts 8:9.
8. Acts 9:43.
9. Luke 7:36–50.
10. Luke 7:44b–46.

How to Use This Resource

You have agreed to serve your church as an usher, greeter, or minister of hospitality. Whatever your parish calls you and however it assigns you tasks, before anything else you are a minister of hospitality. Hospitality is the taproot of your ministry. You will be welcoming people to worship, tending their needs, perhaps helping them find a place, perhaps gathering their gifts during the collection, and bidding them farewell when the service concludes. In every interaction, you will be trying to see each person as Christ does—as a beloved daughter or son of God.

By nature, you are a person who wants to help. You have a deep faith in Christ, a love for the Mass, an interest in people, and a place in a community. You bring many personal gifts to the specific tasks you will take up. And you will be part of something larger. You will help draw people into the community and into Christ's presence in the Mass. Remember the story of the healing of the paralytic?[1] A man who was paralyzed had friends who cared deeply about him and had a profound faith in Christ's power to heal. Even in an over-crowded church, they found a way to place their friend at the feet of Christ—by lowering him through the roof. Of course, all disciples are charged with the mission of bringing people to Christ. But you have chosen to do so by helping them feel welcome and comfortable so they can participate in the liturgy.

About This Resource

This book is about the ministry of hospitality. Because you are a liturgical minister—one who helps the assembly to participate in the Mass—the book will begin by sharing some insights and teachings about the source and summit of Catholic life: the liturgy (chapter 1). It will discuss the theological meanings behind your ministry and some of its history (chapter 2). It will give you practical information and advice about serving as a minister of hospitality, explaining your role throughout the Mass (chapter 3). It will help you think deeply about the spiritual nature of hospitality—as an attitude and way of being—and as an array of services you will offer, even the mundane task of collecting money (chapter 4). Finally, it will provide answers to frequently asked questions, resources for further reading, a glossary of terms, and a prayer for preparing to serve. Throughout the book, you'll find questions for reflection and discussion. This book, whether you read it on your own or as part of a

---

1.   Matthew 9:1–8; Mark 2:1–12; and Luke 5:17–26.

training class, is designed to help you understand what information you need to know and what skills and attitudes you need to cultivate to serve reverently and effectively as a minister of hospitality.

Jesus was frequently a guest. So were his disciples. They all learned that some people welcomed them, while others resisted their arrival. Jesus is still a guest. He is present in the community that gathers for worship.

As a minister of hospitality, if you are on duty when someone enters your church, be on your toes. The next person who enters may be a saint or a sinner. You will know the reputation of many who pass through the door. You will know less about others. You can call some people by name, but not everyone.

As you see people enter, you may be tempted to think that you are more smartly dressed, better informed, more faithful, or more loving. But the ones who love the most are the ones who have been forgiven the most. Each one of us is a sinner, and each one of us is a child of God.

The next person who enters the church will know whether or not you offered genuine hospitality. That person is Christ.

About the Authors

Corinna Laughlin wrote the first chapter, "Your Ministry and the Liturgy." She is the pastoral assistant for liturgy at St. James Cathedral in Seattle, Washington, and liturgy consultant for the Archdiocese of Seattle. She has written extensively on the liturgy for Liturgy Training Publications, an agency of the Archdiocese of Chicago, and has contributed articles to *Pastoral Liturgy*®, *Ministry and Liturgy*, and other publications. She holds a doctorate in English from the University of Washington.

Paul Turner wrote the preface, "The History and Meaning of Your Ministry," and the fourth chapter, "Spirituality and Discipleship." He is the pastor of the Cathedral of the Immaculate Conception in Kansas City, Missouri, and the director of the Office of Divine Worship for the Diocese of Kansas City–St. Joseph. He holds a doctorate in sacred theology from Sant'Anselmo in Rome and is the author of many pastoral and theological resources. He serves as a facilitator for the International Commission on English in the Liturgy.

Karie Ferrell wrote much of chapter 3, the frequently asked questions, resource section, and glossary. She is a graduate of the Parish Liturgy Program, Archdiocese of Chicago, and is working on a master's in divinity at Catholic Theological Union. She has been involved in parish and archdiocesan liturgy for fifteen years, including work in the Archdiocese of Chicago's Office for Divine Worship. She is the director of faith formation at St. Mary's parish in Evanston, Illinois.

Thomas P. Welch, MD, is a psychiatrist and medical director at Sequoia Mental Health Services in Aloha, Oregon, and a spiritual director at the Franciscan Spiritual Center in Milwaukie, Oregon. In addition to an MD from the University of Washington, he has a master's in pastoral ministry from the University of Portland.

Questions for Reflection and Discussion

1. Why have you agreed to serve as an usher or a greeter at your church?

2. What questions do you have about the ministry that you hope this book will answer?

3. Remember a time when you received genuine hospitality. What effect did it have on you?

Chapter One

Your Ministry and the Liturgy

[The liturgy] is the source and summit of the Christian life.

—*Lumen gentium*, 11

You're reading this book because you're thinking about becoming an usher, greeter, or minister of hospitality in your parish. Or perhaps you already serve in this way and are looking for an update or refresher. One thing is certain: you're reading this book because the liturgy matters to you.

What Is Liturgy?

Dictionaries will tell you, in one way or another, that *liturgy* is a collection of rites used in public worship. And that is true. But there is much more to liturgy than that. The word *liturgy* comes from a Greek word meaning "public work" or "work of the people." That hits nearer the mark: liturgy is a special kind of work in which the divine and human come together; we do something, and, more importantly, God does something. Liturgy is not a thing; liturgy is an *event*. So let's ask a different question: What does liturgy *do*?

Liturgy gathers us in the presence of God. In speaking of the Eucharist, the second-century *Didache* emphasizes gathering: "Even as this broken bread was scattered over the hills, and was gathered together and became one, so let Your Church be gathered together from the ends of the earth into Your kingdom."[1] Here the Eucharistic bread, formed from many grains of wheat, is an image of what we are to be: disparate individuals who become something new— a worshiping assembly. In the Bible, the gathering of God's people is

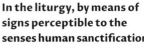

In the liturgy, by means of signs perceptible to the senses human sanctification is signified and brought about in ways proper to each of these signs.

—*Sacrosanctum concilium*, 7[5]

a sign of the in-breaking of the kingdom of God. Think of Isaiah's vision of a great banquet on a mountaintop.[2] Think of Jesus feeding the multitudes[3] or of the disciples gathered in prayer in the upper room on the first Pentecost.[4] When

---

1. *The Didache: The Lord's Teaching Through the Twelve Apostles to the Nations*, 9. http://www.new advent.org/fathers/0714.htm; accessed August 28, 2019.
2. See Isaiah 25:6–9.
3. See Matthew 14:13–21, Mark 6:30-44, Luke 9:10–17, and John 6:1–15.
4. See Acts of the Apostles 2:1–11.
5. This document is also commonly referred to by its English title, the *Constitution on the Sacred Liturgy*. The paragraphs in Church documents are numbered sequentially. The references throughout this resource refer to the corresponding paragraph numbers in the quoted document. Universal Church documents are usually issued first in Latin. Throughout this resource, the Latin titles of these documents have been used. The English titles refer to those documents that are issued by the United States Conference of Catholic Bishops.

Liturgy forms us into community.

God gathers his people together, something happens. The same is true of the liturgy. Before a word has been spoken or a note sung, the liturgy is already a sign of the Kingdom of God because it gathers us together.

Liturgy helps form us into a community. The act of being together at table, of sharing the Word of God, of being one voice in our sung and spoken prayers, has an impact on us. It is through this shared action in the liturgy that we learn to recognize ourselves as a family of believers, the Body of Christ, and to be united in our action outside of the church as well. We join in the liturgy because we are a community, but the reverse is also true: without the liturgy, we are not a community at all.

Liturgy is both common and cosmic. The liturgy takes the most ordinary things—our bodies and voices, light and darkness, water and fire, bread, wine, and oil, time itself—and, through the action of the Holy Spirit, transforms all of these into God's very presence. The liturgy teaches us to see that the entire universe is marked with the presence of Christ. The "seeds" of God are everywhere in the world. The stuff of our holiness is not far away, remote, or arcane. The common is holy.

Christian liturgy is always about the paschal mystery. At the heart of all Christian prayer is the paschal mystery—that is, the life, death, and resurrection of Christ. Whether our prayer is the Mass, the Liturgy of the Hours, a saint's day, a sacrament—whether it is Advent or Christmas Time, Lent, Triduum, or Easter Time—the liturgy is always about the paschal mystery. Why is the paschal mystery so important? Because, in the words of St. Paul, "If Christ has not been raised, your faith is vain; you are still in your sins."[6] The paschal mystery is the fulcrum of history and the dynamic reality which gives meaning to our lives and enlivens our worship. We gather for liturgy in order to be plunged, again and again, into the paschal mystery.

---

6. I Corinthians 15:17.

In the liturgy, we meet Christ. We know that Christ is always close to those who believe: Jesus said, "Whoever loves me will keep my word, and my Father will love him, and we will come to him and make our dwelling with him."[7] But, in the celebration of the Eucharist, Christ is present to us in a special way. In fact, the Church highlights *four* presences of Christ at Mass. Christ is present in the community gathered for prayer; Christ comes to us in each other. Christ is present in the priest, who acts *in persona Christi*, in the person of Christ, in the Mass. Christ is present in the word proclaimed: "When the Sacred Scriptures are read in the Church, God himself speaks to his people, and Christ, present in his word, proclaims the Gospel."[8] And in a unique way, Christ is present in the consecrated bread and wine, his true Body and Blood, shared with us in the Eucharist. Through our participation in this mystery, we meet Christ in many ways and we become what we receive: the Body of Christ.[9]

Liturgy is the worship of the Church. The liturgy is not free-form. As the official prayer of the universal Church, it is governed by universal norms. Most of the texts we hear at Mass—with some significant exceptions, like the homily and the universal prayer—are written down and are the same the world over. Not only the words of liturgy, but most of the actions are the same everywhere: standing, sitting, and kneeling. The liturgical books include many rubrics (from the Latin word for "red," because these instructions are sometimes printed in red ink), which give instructions for how and where each part of the liturgy happens. All of this should remind us that the liturgy does not belong to any one person, priest, or parish. The liturgy is the Church's prayer. But that does not mean that it is not *our* prayer too. In the words of the Second Vatican Council, the liturgy is "the outstanding means whereby the faithful may express in their lives and manifest to others the mystery of Christ and the real nature of the true Church."[10] Liturgy is our means of expression with Christ and about Christ. In other words, liturgy is the language we speak as Catholics.

> The preeminent manifestation of the Church is present in the full, active participation of all God's holy people in these liturgical celebrations, especially in the same eucharist.
>
> —*Sacrosanctum concilium*, 41

The liturgy is richly varied. While the liturgy is carefully governed by liturgical books, it is never monotone. It is constantly changing, with different readings for every day of the year, and different prayers for most days. Through the liturgical year, the Church invites us to meditate on different aspects of the mystery of Christ, from his conception to his Second Coming. The liturgy is colorful!

---

7. John 14:23.
8. *General Instruction of the Roman Missal* (GIRM), 29.
9. See SC, 7.
10. SC, 2.

The Eucharist is the most important of the Church's liturgies, but it is not our only liturgy. The liturgies of the Church also include rites like those in the *Rite of Christian Initiation of Adults* and the *Order of Christian Funerals*. They include celebrations of the other sacraments, from baptism, confirmation, and Eucharist to anointing and penance, matrimony, and holy orders. In addition, the Liturgy of the Hours, prayed daily by deacons, priests, bishops, religious, and many laypeople, is part of the Church's liturgy, sanctifying the hours of each day with prayer to God.

Liturgy is different from devotion. The Church has a rich and wonderful array of devotional prayer—novenas, chaplets, the Rosary, the Way of the Cross, among others—which can enrich our prayer and bring us closer to Christ and to his Mother. The Rosary has a special place in the life of the Church, for, in the words of St. John Paul II, it "serves as an excellent introduction and a faithful echo of the Liturgy, enabling people to participate fully and interiorly in it and to reap its fruits in their daily lives."[11] These devotions can enrich, but must never replace, our participation in the liturgy.

Liturgy both reflects and shapes our faith. A medieval scholar expressed this in a phrase that has become famous: *lex orandi, lex credendi*, which can loosely be translated as "the law of prayer shapes the law of belief." In other words, the way we pray informs our theology. If you look at the footnotes in the documents of the Second Vatican Council, and in the *Catechism of the Catholic Church*, you'll notice that the sources cited for key teachings not only include the Bible and teachings of popes and councils, but prayers from the Mass. Liturgy is a school of prayer and a school of faith, teaching us to believe with the Church.

The medieval adage is often extended to read *lex orandi, lex credendi, lex vivendi*—"law of life." The way we pray shapes what we believe—and the way we live our lives. Authentic worship and faith lead to discipleship. If it doesn't, it means the transforming power of the liturgy is not really reaching us. As Pope Benedict XVI has written, "A Eucharist which does not pass over into the concrete practice of love is intrinsically fragmented."[12]

Liturgy really matters. *Sacrosanctum concilium* of the Second Vatican Council had this to say about liturgy: "The liturgy is the summit toward which the activity of the Church is directed; at the same time it is the font from which all her power flows."[13] Liturgy is both source and summit, culmination and starting-place. All the preaching and evangelizing the Church does is meant to draw people to Christ in the celebration of the Eucharist. At the same time, though, the Eucharist is not a stopping place. Liturgy is the fountain from which we draw strength to do Christ's work in the world. Liturgy gathers us;

---

11. *Rosarium Virginis Mariae*, 4.
12. *Deus caritas est*, 14.
13. SC, 10.

liturgy also sends us forth. And if liturgy fails to do that, there is a problem. "We cannot delude ourselves," wrote St. John Paul II, "by our mutual love and, in particular, by our concern for those in need we will be recognized as true followers of Christ. . . . This will be the criterion by which the authenticity of our Eucharistic celebrations is judged."[14]

The Privilege to Serve

Liturgical ministers have the wonderful privilege of helping others to participate in this transforming reality we call the Church's liturgy. Whether we are proclaiming a Scripture

Ministers of hospitality have the privilege of welcoming and hosting.

reading, taking up the collection, distributing Communion, carrying a candle, or preparing the liturgical environment, our goal is the same: to help others find in the liturgy what we have found—a community of believers, a school of holiness, a place of encounter with Jesus Christ. When we go to Mass, we never come out the same, because liturgy is meant to change us. No wonder, then that the Church puts such emphasis on participation in the liturgy. If we participate fully, consciously, and actively in the liturgy, we cannot fail to be transformed, and do our part to transform the world we live in. As liturgical ministers, we are called to do just that, and to help others do the same.

Questions for Reflection and Discussion

1. How is praying with a community different than praying on your own? Why do you think Jesus calls us to pray in both ways?

2. What liturgies of the Church do you participate in on a regular basis?

3. Where and when do you feel closest to Christ?

4. Think about the ways Christ is present in the liturgy and in the world. Think of a time when you have felt Christ's presence in these places.

5. Do you find that participating in the liturgy has an impact on your life outside of the liturgy?

---

14. *Mane nobiscum Domine*, 28.

Chapter Two

The Meaning and History of Your Ministry

Welcome one another, then, as Christ welcomed you,
for the glory of God.

—Romans 15:7

In this blessing of liturgical ministers, the *Book of Blessings* assumes that ushers serve as greeters in addition to their other duties: "By virtue of our baptism in Christ some of us are called to serve as ministers of the liturgical assembly: . . . ushers provide welcome and dignified order to the celebration. . . ."[1] In many parishes, ushers are not necessarily greeters, and greeters are not necessarily ushers, but both are ministers of hospitality. You may be asked to perform one or both of these roles, but whatever specific tasks you are given, you will want to be attentive to the needs of the assembly members throughout the worship time, responding with the reverence and order appropriate to the liturgy.

Ushers Past and Present

Within recent memory, Catholic churches used ushers more than greeters. Ushers were easy to stereotype: They were men. They wore suits. They had a room in the back of the church where they left their coats and congregated before Mass. If they didn't have a separate room, they draped a chain across the back pew and hung a sign there: USHERS ONLY. They rang the church bell.

As people entered the church, ushers would find them a place. Some people arrived early enough that they did not require assistance. But as the time for Mass drew near, places started to fill, and ushers got busier. They started patrolling the center and side aisles. They looked for places large enough to accommodate various sizes of newly arriving groups.

In the final minutes before Mass, the pace intensified. People had rushed to get to church on time, and they stepped inside a bit dazed. They sized up the situation as best they could. They had made it to church before Mass had begun, but they needed a place to sit, and openings were hard to spot.

Ushers, though, were visible. Their faces sometimes even a bit stern, they would stand in full view, catch the eye of those just arriving, and gesticulate like traffic cops—but without the whistle. One arm would make robust circles inviting the unseated worshippers forward. The hand on the other arm would

---

1. *Book of Blessings*, 1858.

6

hold up the number of fingers indicating an opening for one, two, or three people. Those already in the partly available pew scrunched over to make more room. The usher would nod his head approvingly, return his gaze to the folks standing in the back of the church, and increase the number of raised fingers.

Those who scrunched over, invariably opened up places *in the middle* of the pew, not on the aisles. Aisle seating has long been the premium seating in Catholic churches. People who care about where they sit still arrive very early to claim a seat on the aisle—or even in the back. (Theatergoers arrive early to get front seats, but churchgoers arrive early to sit in the back.) If somebody wants to enter the pew, that is fine with those already there, but new arrivals take seats in the middle. The owners of aisle seats let them sidestep through the narrow space between their knees and the back of the pew in front of them. A moment's inconvenience at the start of Mass is better than giving up the aisle seat for an entire Mass. Throughout recent history, an usher could get people into seats, but no usher would succeed in moving a seated worshipper off the aisle.

Once Mass began, the ushers would stay in the back. As latecomers arrived, ushers would still seat them. Ushers would walk back up the aisle for this purpose even when Mass had begun. As they understood it, the seating of worshippers was more important than anything else happening in the church. It took precedence over singing the opening hymn and the first words of the priest from the sanctuary.

As Mass continued, ushers would remain standing near the vestibule. Even if people stopped coming in, some would visit quietly with one another, walk around at the back, stare out the door, or check their watches.

When it came time for the collection, ushers would go back into action. They would grab the baskets, process to the front of the church, and start taking up the collection pew by pew to the rear. There they would bag it. In some churches they counted it immediately.

When it was time for Communion, ushers would go to the front of the church again and invite people out of their pew. They would stand just behind a pew, let its inhabitants exit, and direct them to Communion. The next pew would not begin to exit until the usher had given them permission. Ushers walked slowly backward, row by row, until everyone had received Communion. Then they themselves would receive last.

At the end of the service, ushers passed out bulletins to all as they left. They would pick up their coats, tidy up the space in the back of the church, and wend their way home after another Sunday Mass.

Admittedly, that portrait of the formidable usher is a stereotype. Even the most regimented usher of the past was a man of faith. He wanted to serve the Church, and he did it the way he was trained. He cared about people and wanted to help them. He wanted them to feel at home in church and to leave with the information they needed to live out their faith another week. Ushers were the pillars of a parish Church. They held baskets for the collection because they were the most trustworthy members of the community. They deserve our respect and thanks.

Over time, our needs have shifted. In the past, people coming to church needed a place to sit, a basket for their gift, a cue for Communion, and a bulletin to take home. Ushers helped people at Mass do everything they needed to do.

Now we encourage people to do more. We want them to form a community by visiting with their friends in faith before and after the service. We want them to join in the singing and to pay full attention to the proclamation of the Scriptures. We want everyone to participate: the priest, the deacon, the ministers, the servers, the choir, the people—and the ushers. Everyone comes for this purpose: to participate at Mass. All the ministers, including the ushers, should give a good example.

The role of the usher has changed because the role of the people has changed. Some parishes have therefore changed the title of these ministers from "ushers" to "greeters," while other parishes have added greeting to the list of an usher's duties. Still, other parishes call people who fulfill these functions "ministers of hospitality." These shifts emphasize different responsibilities. Ushers and greeters are not traffic cops helping people move safely and quickly to the right spot. They are hosts who put a face onto the parish. They welcome those who arrive and begin the process of forming them as a worshiping body.

The *General Instruction of the Roman Missal* names these roles among those fulfilled by liturgical ministers at Mass:

c. Those who take up the collections in the church.

d. Those who, in some regions, welcome the faithful at the church doors, seat them appropriately, and marshal them in processions.[2]

With these changes in roles has also come a change in space. Many older Catholic churches have very little space between the front door and the back pew. This vestibule was large enough for people to catch their breath before taking a seat, but insufficient for congregating prior to the service. Many newer churches include a narthex or gathering space where people can visit. When people walk in, they seem to spontaneously know how to use this area. But having greeters on duty will help. All who enter should feel the sense of Christian welcome. When people have begun forming the community before the start of Mass, they are better prepared to join in the community's activities of singing, speaking, listening, and observing silence together.

---

2. GIRM, 105.

Ministers of hospitality welcome people and begin the process of forming them into community.

Are you an usher, a greeter, or both? It depends on what your parish asks of you, and on your personal gifts. No matter what your title is, your parish will be grateful that you want to serve God by helping those who gather for Sunday Mass.

Evangelization

When you greet people coming to church, you evangelize. Many Catholics think of evangelization as something that other Christians do. We don't go door to door asking people if they know Jesus Christ. We don't send out bulk emails or activate automated phone calls. Traditionally we Catholics are happy to share our faith, but we usually wait for the other person to make the first move.

Pope Paul VI wrote that the Church exists in order to evangelize. Evangelization is "the carrying forth of the Good News to every sector of the human race," where it will bring strength and renewal.[3] We all share this responsibility of bringing Christ to others. Pope Francis writes that Christians "should appear as people who wish to share their joy, . . . who invite others to a delicious banquet."[4]

When you serve as a greeter at your church, you are still not making the first move in evangelization. Something has already prompted people to come to the door. Most are coming because they are members who have attended

---

3. *Evangelii nuntiandi* (*On Evangelization in the Modern World*), Paul VI, Apostolic Exhortation, 1975, 14 and 18.
4. *Evangelii gaudium* (*The Joy of the Gospel*), Francis, Apostolic Exhortation, 2013, 14.

Ministers of hospitality are people who wish to share their joy.

for many years. Some come less frequently. Others are visitors. But some few are checking out a Catholic church for the first time in their lives. The Spirit has moved their hearts, and they have taken a big step. Now it's your turn. You are the face of Christ, and your welcome will evangelize.

St. Benedict wrote a rule of life for those who wanted to live as monks. He expected these dedicated men to form a religious community. But they were not to live in complete isolation. They had to be ready to welcome the visitor. When some visitors come at inopportune times, their presence may feel like an intrusion on one's home. But Benedict wanted his monasteries to be known for this virtue: hospitality. He wanted monks to welcome *all* guests and to have the right attitude toward them. Some people merely tolerated guests. Benedict had another idea. "All guests who present themselves are to be welcomed as Christ, for he himself will say: *I was a stranger and you welcomed me* (Matthew 25:35)."[5] When you are a greeter at church, you are the face of Christ, and you are receiving each guest as if he or she were Christ.

In fact, they are. Jesus said that wherever two or three are gathered in his name, he is there in the midst of them.[6] So when we gather for worship, "Christ is really present in the very liturgical assembly gathered in his name."[7] We greet Christ in one another long before we receive him in the sacrament of Communion.

---

5. From chapter 53 in *RB 1980: The Rule of St. Benedict in Latin and English with Notes*, edited by Timothy Fry, OSB (Collegeville, MN: Liturgical Press, 1981), 25–27.

6. Matthew 18:20.

7. GIRM, 27.

Porters

A distant ancestor to the usher is the porter, or doorkeeper. Back in the Middle Ages, long before electricity, wristwatches, and smartphones, the porter rang the church bell to announce the start of Mass. The porter also unlocked the church and prepared the liturgical books and the sacristy. The same person was to help keep order, letting worshippers in and keeping troublemakers out.

A thousand years ago, certain men were trusted with the keys of the church in a solemn ceremony over which the bishop presided. One minister instructed the candidates about their responsibilities, and the bishop offered a prayer for them. By the thirteenth century, the new porter tried out the keys and the bell right in the middle of this elaborate ritual.

This ceremony became absorbed into those required for a man to be ordained a priest. "Porter" was one of the minor orders, just as priesthood was one of the major orders. In time, the only ones being made porters were those who were studying for the priesthood.

Pope Paul VI abolished the ceremony for porters in 1972 because it had lost its meaning. The keys to a parish church were being entrusted to plenty of people who would never be ordained priests, men and women alike. In an effort to focus the ceremonies leading up to ordination to the priesthood, Paul VI discontinued the one for porters.

Today, a simpler ceremony has been included in the American edition of the *Book of Blessings*.[8] It is not required of anyone who wishes to serve the church as an usher, but it gives the parish a way to pray over those it appoints to this task. The pastor normally gives the blessing, but another priest or a deacon may do so.

Helping People Participate

Whether you see yourself as an usher or a greeter, your ministry is to welcome people and help them participate at Mass—and that begins with providing a model of participation. Your responsibilities may be limited to finding seats for people and taking up the collection, or you may be more of a goodwill ambassador, or even a sergeant at arms. But remember, you come to church first to worship, and then to serve. In your ministry, by attending reverently to the liturgy, you help others worship too.

> **Their purpose is to ensure that the faithful, who come together as one, establish communion and dispose themselves properly to listen to the Word of God and to celebrate the Eucharist worthily.**
>
> —General Instruction of the Roman Missal, 46

You are already familiar with the Mass, but take a closer look at the parts where you may play a key role. The more you understand how the parts of the

---

8. BB, 1847–1870.

Mass fit together, the better you will pray at church, and the better you will serve those who meet you there.

Introductory Rites

Mass begins with the Introductory Rites. These start with the entrance of the ministers and end just before the readings. The assembly is invited to stand throughout the introductory rites.

Ushers and greeters work toward the goal of introductory rites even before Mass begins. From the moment people arrive at church, they are to "come together as one," "establish communion," and "dispose themselves . . . to listen" to the readings. You are in a unique position to help. When you greet people with a friendly face, you are already helping establish the communion that is so essential for the first part of the Mass.

You will naturally want to greet your friends. But your ministry is to the entire community. If you greet only your friends, you do not build up the entire Body of Christ; you segment it. When you hold open the door for everyone, you make each worshipper feel a part of the whole body. When you greet even those you do not know, you show the concern of Christ for each member of the flock. When you learn the names of those who come to church, you strengthen the bond among the faithful.

Ushers and greeters can also help people meet people. You aren't the only one who may have trouble remembering names. Everyone at church faces the same challenge. When you introduce one worshipper to another, you weave the fabric of a strong celebration.

Having a variety of ushers and greeters will make this welcoming easier to achieve. The old and the young, men and women, people of various races and ancestry—having representatives from all these groups among the greeters will help ensure that no one who arrives feels alone.

As people enter, they may need you to do more than welcome them. They may have questions and specific needs. Be ready to receive donations for the food pantry, push a wheelchair, direct people to restrooms, or explain how to contact a staff member. All these actions form community.

> For in the readings, as explained by the Homily, God speaks to his people, opening up to them the mystery of redemption and salvation, and offering spiritual nourishment; and Christ himself is present through his word in the midst of the faithful.
>
> —General Instruction of the Roman Missal, 55

In addition, people entering into a large gathering, especially for the first time, are reassured to recognize someone who can answer questions and attend to needs. Having seen you in action at the beginning of Mass, they know there will be someone to turn to if a need arises later.

Once people are in their seats, they continue to dispose themselves to listen to God's Word and share the Eucharist. They typically spend some time in private prayer. If you command too much attention in the aisles before Mass and during the introductory rites, you distract the faithful from their spiritual purpose. All of your actions need to be reverent and modest.

Good ushers and greeters build up the entire Body of Christ. They multiply the number of people they get to know at church. They welcome people and help them find seats. They are easy to identify. They will not, however, draw undue attention to themselves or limit their welcome to those they know.

The Liturgy of the Word

The first main part of the Mass is the Liturgy of the Word, in which passages from the Bible are proclaimed for all to hear and heed.

You come to Mass first to participate, then to serve as an usher or greeter. So your main task during the Liturgy of the Word is to listen. Your attention will give a good example to others.

Some parishes ask ushers not to seat latecomers during the proclamation of the Scriptures. A parallel custom is observed in some other places of business. At theaters, for example, latecomers are seated between scenes, and sometimes out of view, so they do not disturb those who arrived on time. If you hold people at the door for any reason, be sure to treat them charitably, and demonstrate for them the appropriate action: observe silence as much as possible and focus your attention on the Word of God. In this way you show respect for God and for the people who are hearing the divine Word.

Disturbances are bound to happen. Ushers and greeters may need to help whenever something unusual happens. In whatever you do, act charitably. The way you act should be consistent with the message people hear in the Scripture: love one another, as God has loved you.

Liturgy of the Eucharist

The second main part of the Mass is the Liturgy of the Eucharist. Here the faithful share in the sacrifice and banquet of Jesus Christ. The Liturgy of the Eucharist has three sections.

a. At the preparation of the gifts, bread and the wine with water are brought to the altar, the same elements, that is to say, which Christ took into his hands.

> The Christian faithful are obliged to assist with the needs of the Church so that the Church has what is necessary for divine worship, for the works of the apostolate and of charity, and for the decent support of ministers.
>
> —Code of Canon Law, 222 §1

b. In the Eucharistic Prayer, thanks is given to God for the whole work of salvation, and the offerings become the Body and Blood of Christ.

c. Through the fraction and through Communion, the faithful, though many, receive from the one bread the Lord's Body and from the one chalice the Lord's Blood in the same way the apostles received them from the hands of Christ himself.[9]

The collection takes place during the first of these sections, and ushers make it flow smoothly. The collection is not an intermission; it connects with the other sections of the Liturgy of the Eucharist.

People are expected to contribute to the support of the parish Church.

In times past, people brought their own bread and wine as gifts for the local Church. The collection of gifts has always indicated the peoples' willingness to share with others what God has given them. To express this communal offering more fully, many parishes ask the ushers to invite several people from the assembly to bring the gifts forward.

This collection has the practical purpose of helping the parish pay its bills. But it also has spiritual significance. In offering their gifts, people are offering themselves. The gifts of bread and wine will be transformed into the Body and Blood of Christ, and the people who share Communion will be transformed as well.

The people offer their gifts for the support of the parish and symbolically offer themselves to be transformed.

For this reason, the collection of the gifts is a prelude to what people will do during the Eucharistic Prayer. Many Catholics assume their role in the Eucharistic Prayer is to be quiet while the priest recites a long text. However, they are to take the next logical step after contributing their gifts.

A circular action takes place at every Mass. The people bring their gifts to be placed on the altar as a sign of their very selves. The gifts and the people are transformed through the power of the Holy Spirit. Then the people receive the transformed gifts of bread and wine, now the Body and Blood of Christ, in holy Communion. After Mass, their financial offerings will allow the Church to continue its ministry. The people give, and the people receive. When the ushers gather the collection and arrange for it to be brought forward, they are helping people make their sacrifice and get ready to receive the Body and Blood of Christ. The impact of the offering extends beyond Mass to the work of the Church in the world.

On some Sundays the Catholic community takes up a second collection for a specific need. Many parishes schedule this collection after Communion, but if it takes place immediately after the first collection, the spiritual

---

9. GIRM, 72.

significance of this offering is easier to grasp. We give all our gifts as a sign of our sacrifice, and the Holy Spirit responds with the greatest gift of all, Communion in Christ.

Concluding Rites

Once the Communion Rite is over, Mass concludes with announcements, a blessing, and the dismissal. As people leave the church, ministers of hospitality help again. You hold open the doors and pass out bulletins or other items of information. You bid people goodbye.

You are helping people make the transition from worship into service. You send them forth renewed in Christ, looking for ways to bring Christ to a waiting world. The bulletins you give them signify their mission. They are not just leaving the building; they are entering the world. A Church could fittingly hang this sign over the exit: SERVICE ENTRANCE. You help people take the Gospel with them.

> The meaning of this [Eucharistic] Prayer is that the whole congregation of the faithful joins with Christ in confessing the great deeds of God and in the offering of Sacrifice. The Eucharistic Prayer requires that everybody listen to it with reverence and in silence.
>
> —General Instruction of the Roman Missal, 78

Other Liturgies

Ministers of hospitality are very helpful at Sunday Mass, but they are needed for other liturgies as well. Many guests are on hand at weddings, funerals, baptisms, and confirmations. Some of them will be visitors unfamiliar with the parish or with Catholic worship. Ushers and greeters who are welcoming and attentive will help everyone feel at home and participate. Consider also penance services.

Questions for Reflection and Discussion

1. How did you first become interested in becoming an usher or a greeter?

2. When have you received an especially warm welcome? Was it at church or in some other place? What made it memorable?

3. When you come to church, what sacrifice are you offering?

4. When you exit the doors of the church, what mission are you beginning?

Chapter Three

Serving as a Minister of Hospitality

I was . . . a stranger and you welcomed me.

—Matthew 25:35

A Ministry of Hospitality

Ministers of hospitality recognize the face of Christ in the faces of people who come through the door.

As ministers of hospitality, you will be cultivating a welcoming attitude and learning how to discern the needs of the people you welcome. As you've already read, the friendliness and kindness you express are not simply social skills; they grow out of a recognition of the face of Christ in the faces of the people who come through the door. In order to put genuine Christian love into action, there are things you will need to know and skills you will need to practice.

What Ushers and Greeters Need to Know

Expect to encounter every possible need or question. Here are some topics you will want to learn about.

Know the Layout of Your Parish's Physical Plant

Although most of the people who arrive at the church door will be coming for liturgy, some may be trying to find another location on your church campus. A neighbor may be dropping off a child for religious education classes, parents may be looking for a baptism preparation class, volunteers may be expecting to help out at a Knights of Columbus pancake breakfast, or an inquirer may be trying to find the first meeting for the Rite of Christian Initiation of Adults (RCIA). Your knowledge of the buildings and grounds will help you direct them to the right building and let them know where to enter. Be familiar with the locations of the school, the parish offices, the rectory, and the parish hall, and be able to direct people to the entrances if the buildings are open during Mass times.

Know the Parking Rules

The church parking lot on Sunday morning can be one of the most difficult tests of our love for one another. Your ability to help people find the right lot, to point out illegal or reserved spaces, and to let people know about particular customs (everyone exits or enters in a particular direction, one-way lanes, and so forth) will help to make things run more smoothly as people arrive and depart. If your parish is in an urban setting, know the parking rules on the street. Do people need a sticker to park on certain streets? Is it permissible to park on certain streets, but only during certain hours on Sunday mornings or Saturday evenings? Are some places on the street illegal for parking during Mass times to allow for drop-off and pick up of persons with disabilities?

Know the Interior Layout of the Church

Know where all the restrooms are located, which ones have facilities for changing babies, and which ones are accessible to people in wheelchairs. Are there men's rooms and women's rooms, or are they unisex? Where can you find restroom supplies if needed? Where is drinking water available? Is there a coatroom? Where is the lost and found?

Be able to direct altar servers, other ministers, and visiting priests to the sacristy. Know the policy on purchasing candles for lighting and whether there are shrines or altars dedicated to particular saints. What is represented in the sculpture, stained glass windows, or other decorative art in the church? Where is daily Mass celebrated? Is there a Blessed Sacrament chapel adjacent to the sanctuary, or is the tabernacle in the sanctuary?

Make the effort to sit in varying areas of your parish's worship space so that you'll be able to guide people to seating that meets their needs. Which pews have the best sight lines for people with small children, proximity to the restrooms or to the cry room? Are there hot spots or cold spots or areas where the sound system doesn't project well?

Where can people in wheelchairs find space without feeling conspicuous? Pews with kneelers can be difficult to navigate for people with canes. Is there seating in your parish that addresses this issue? Does your parish offer signing for people with hearing disabilities? Where should they sit in order to see?

Especially in urban settings, people may come to your church door seeking social services. Your parish should be prepared for this need with information about what the parish offers and how to access it. It would also be hospitable to offer a list of other services in your area—numbers to call or nearby places to go that offer food, shelter, and other aid.

Know Your Parish Staff

Know the names of your pastor, the associate pastors, deacons, and lay staff members. Check the schedule or ask in the rectory or parish office to learn who is celebrating and assisting at the day's liturgies. Does the celebrant stay afterward to greet the congregation? Where will he be? How can people contact the staff during the week?

There are lots of people who minister in the parish. Get to know their names and what they do. Is there a pastoral associate or a director of religious education on staff? Who directs the choir? Do any deacons minister in your parish? Who is the contact for parents seeking baptism for their children? Who coordinates the process for initiating adults into the faith (sometimes called the catechumenate or RCIA—Rite of Christian Initiation of Adults)? Whom should a couple call to make arrangements to be married? Keep your parish bulletin on hand or keep your own list of the parish's pastoral ministers with their office phone numbers (including extensions), so that you can direct people with inquiries to the appropriate person.

Know What to Do in Case of an Emergency

Parishes need to anticipate all sorts of emergencies: medical, fire, natural disaster, even someone armed intending to do harm. Your parish should have a plan for these emergencies, developed in consultation with experts. Learn it and follow it.

Carry your cell phone with you at all times in case you need to summon emergency services. Know the exact physical address of the church and the nearest cross street so you can provide this information to the first responders.

Know where the emergency exits are and how to facilitate the evacuation of the building if necessary. You should know the locations of all the fire extinguishers and how to use them.

Where are first aid supplies kept? Is there a defibrillator in the building? Who knows how to use it? Take a first aid course—whether or not your parish requires it. The skills you'll learn may save someone's life, and the confidence you'll gain may help you to be a cool head in the event of a serious emergency.

Know Your Responsibilities for Child and Youth Protection

Several companies provide best practices programs for protecting children and youth in Catholic institutions. This training is usually required for employees, volunteers, and parents in parishes, Catholic schools, and diocesan offices. All parish personnel, paid or volunteer, who work with children or youth should be certified through this program in order for the parish to be in compliance with its requirements.

Check with your parish coordinator to find out whether your parish requires ushers and greeters to go through this process. Whether or not it is required, the Church benefits when as many as possible of its ministers are trained.

As ushers and greeters, you will be in a unique position to be aware of potentially dangerous situations for children and youth. Everyone wants to assume that people are safe in church. You can do your part to make that a reality by knowing what kinds of behaviors are inappropriate and what areas of the buildings might be secluded enough to present a danger.

Know How to Participate in the Liturgy

While you have specific duties before, during, and after the liturgy, your most important duty is the same as that of all the gathered assembly—to participate fully and consciously in the liturgy. Know when to stand, kneel, and sit; know and make the appropriate gestures; learn the responses; raise your voice in song. Like all of the other liturgical ministers, part of your ministry is a ministry of example for those people who come to Mass unsure about what to do. Most important, try to enter into the spirit and meaning of the liturgy. Christ is speaking to his people in the readings. The people are responding in the responsorial psalm. They are offering their lives as they offer their gifts. The Lord feeds the people with his body and blood and then sends them out into the world to announce the Gospel.

All of us need support in our ministries. The other volunteer and professional ministers and the clergy need yours. When you know the liturgy and participate in it with genuine reverence and assurance in your role, you support the role of others. When you know when to move and what to do, you free other ministers to perform their duties without needing to be concerned about you and yours. When we all do our part, we are all free to enter into the liturgy in a prayerful way.

Because you are a liturgical minister, and others will look to you as a model, it is especially important to review how to receive Communion. The United States Conference of Catholic Bishops has instructed us to first bow our heads as a gesture of reverence as we approach the minister of Communion to receive holy Communion, either under one species or under both. Then the minister holds up the Eucharistic bread or the chalice containing the precious blood and says, "The Body of Christ" or "The Blood of Christ." We respond by saying, "Amen." If we wish to receive the host on the tongue, we open our mouths and slightly extend the tongue. If we wish to receive in the hand, we hold out our slightly cupped hands, one above the other. When the Eucharist is placed in the hand, we take one step to the side, pick up the Host with the lower hand, and consume it. If we are receiving from the chalice, the minister presents it to us; we say, "Amen," take it in our hands to drink from it, and return it carefully to the minister.

Because it is at the altar that the memorial of the Lord is celebrated and his Body and Blood given to the faithful, it came to pass that the Church's writers see in the altar a sign of Christ himself — hence the saying arose: "The altar is Christ."

—Order of the Dedication of a Church and Altar, chapter 4, number 4

If you are uncertain about what to do and when to do it in the liturgy, ask your coordinator to provide some formation sessions to help you. You're probably not the only one. Also, use references readily available to you for help. Most hymnals include an Order of Mass with all of the responses, and missals give a very detailed "tour" of the Mass. Although the ideal is to learn your role by heart and not be focused on a book throughout the liturgy, such aids can help you prepare and give you support until you know your part well. There are many other resources that can deepen your experience of the Mass. Check the Resources chapter of this book for suggestions.

Know How to Move Reverently throughout the Sacred Space of the Church

Although your duties begin at the entrances to the church, you may be moving to various places throughout the building as you help people find a place to sit, assist with processions, or take up the collection. You need to know how to reverence the sacred places appropriately so that you can model reverent behavior for the assembly.

When you come to the front of the church before taking up the collection, make a profound bow to the altar.

All our movements in the church building should be dignified and reverent, but there are two sacred places that require special attention: the altar and the tabernacle. When approaching the altar or passing in front of it, we reverence it with a profound bow from the waist.

The tabernacle is a solid cabinet in which the Blessed Sacrament is reserved for the sick, for *viaticum* (holy Communion before death), and for prayer and meditation. Traditionally, a lamp nearby is kept lit "to indicate the presence of Christ and honor it."[1] The tabernacle may be located in the sanctuary, or it may be placed nearby in a chapel.[2] When approaching or passing in front of a tabernacle outside of Mass (not during Mass), we genuflect by bending the right knee to the ground as an expression of adoration.[3] Remember that during Mass we do not genuflect to the tabernacle. Our focus at that time is on the altar. When going about your duties, keep in mind these two different postures for reverencing altar and tabernacle, the deep bow and the genuflection. For example, when taking up the collection, most ushers walk to the front of the church with the collection baskets and work backward. At the front of the church, before the altar, you would make a profound bow before turning to begin the collection.

---

1. GIRM, 316.
2. GIRM, 314–315; *Built of Living Stones*, 70–80.
3. GIRM, 274.

Skills to Develop

Attentiveness

Ushers and greeters must be attentive to the needs of the members of the assembly and to the actions of the liturgy. This may take time to develop. Find your own process for disconnecting from the busyness and distractions of your daily life before coming to Mass, so that you can be present to the liturgy and your fellow worshippers.

Effective Communication

Combine steady eye contact and sincere words to share the love of Christ with all of God's people who cross the church threshold. Make the effort to greet everyone. Smile.

Crowd Control

Develop methods for directing people that are compatible with your personality strengths. Your usher or greeter name tag or badge will help establish your role. Courtesy goes a long way—remember to say please and thank you as you encourage people to move up or move in, guide them away from reserved seating, or ask them to wait for the procession to pass before they find their seat.

Compassion

People come to church with a variety of challenges. You cannot tell just by looking at people how much mental or emotional distress they might be carrying. They might have just lost a loved one or been laid off from a job. They may be struggling with a mental illness or addiction. They may be the primary caretaker of a loved one and coming to church is the only break they get. They might have suffered any number of traumas. Your calm presence and caring smile can be healing or even transformative to the person whose initial response to you might be unfriendly, curt, or even rude. Do not take their reactions personally; they might be doing the best they can in their current situation. Instead, reflect back to them the loving face of Christ.

Responsibilities of Ushers and Greeters

Some parishes have ushers and some have greeters; some parishes have both. The responsibilities may differ from parish to parish.

As you read through this section, be sure that you know what your role is, which responsibilities are yours, and how to fulfill them. If you're not sure, contact your coordinator to see if there is a written job description or a set of guidelines. If there isn't, use what follows as an outline for a discussion so that one can be developed.

Before the Liturgy

Your coordinator will tell you how early you are expected to arrive. If you are responsible for tidying the building before the people arrive, this will have to be well before Mass time.

YOUR APPEARANCE

Personal hygiene and attire: Be sure clothes are clean, neat, and appropriate. Clothing should not be too revealing, and it should show respect for yourself and for your role in the liturgical life of the Church. Perhaps your parish has a dress code for its ministers.

Badge or name tag: Your parish should provide a badge or name tag to identify you as an usher or greeter. Be sure you wear it and that it's visible to others.

APPEARANCE OF THE ENTRYWAYS, GATHERING SPACE, AND WORSHIP SPACE

Entrances to the building: Your parish may have maintenance personnel on duty on Sundays, but perhaps not. If it's necessary and you're able, sweep leaves or shovel snow, and sprinkle salt on icy steps and walkways. Be sure that nothing is obstructing the entryways, such as tables set up for ticket sales. Straighten floor mats so that they are not tripping hazards.

Indoor areas: It never hurts to tidy up. Straighten the pamphlet racks and bulletin boards. Pick up left-behind personal items and trash. Lift kneelers. Check that the baskets for the collection are out and placed in a convenient spot.

Restrooms: Cleanliness here should go without saying. Also, be sure there are toilet paper, towels, and soap, and that the diaper changing station is in working order and clean.

Reserved seating: Check to see if any areas need to be reserved, and make sure they're designated in a clearly visible way. Be sure to remove reserved seating signs from the previous liturgy if they're no longer needed.

Temperature: Is it too cold, drafty, or too hot inside the building? Know the policies regarding who has access to the thermostats and whether windows should be opened.

As the Assembly Gathers

KNOW YOUR STATION

Which entrance is your responsibility? Are you to be standing outside or inside the doors? Are there greeters in the parking lots? Is anyone designated to help at the coat racks or in a coat room?

THE OUTDOOR STATION

If your parish stations greeters in the parking lot (or on the sidewalks in urban settings), consider your job similar to that of the ushers who assist people in finding seats. Help drivers navigate the parking areas. Point out the parking spaces designated for people with disabilities, let people know about available spaces in an alternate lot or if space has just opened up near the building. Direct traffic if things become congested. Be mindful of the safety of small children. In inclement weather, you could be the smiling person with a large umbrella or a steady arm for a senior on an icy day.

WELCOMING THE PEOPLE

Welcome each person. Greet everyone with a smile and, if appropriate, a hand-shake, if possible. As it gets busier, acknowledge everyone with a smile and eye contact. It may be tempting to converse with the people you know well, but remember that you're there to help everyone feel welcome.

DISTRIBUTE WORSHIP AIDS OR OTHER ITEMS NEEDED FOR FULL PARTICIPATION IN THE LITURGY

Worship aids are designed to enable people to participate well—to sing, respond, and generally follow along. It's vital that all are equipped to participate when they take their seats. On some occasions they will need other items, such as palms on Palm Sunday and tapers at the Easter Vigil. You will be responsible for distributing these as well.

CHOOSE PEOPLE TO CARRY THE GIFTS OF BREAD AND WINE

Make the effort to offer this opportunity to many different members of the community. It can be tempting to ask the same people from week to week—to rely on the people you know well or who often sit in the most convenient place, but resist that temptation. Ask families with children, couples, single people, senior members of the community, people with disabilities (assuming that they can carry the gifts comfortably and safely), teens, men and women, people of all colors and ethnicities. If you make this request as people gather, you'll have the time to give them some instruction. Will an usher come to escort them from their pew, or do they need a cue so they know when to move? What do they do when they get to the foot of the sanctuary? Be sure you know how to instruct them to make them feel at ease.

Inviting members of the assembly to present the gifts highlights the community's participation.

OFFER TO SEAT PEOPLE WHEN THEY SEEM UNSURE OR IF THE CHURCH IS CROWDED

Placement: Encourage people to sit near each other and to fill in the front pews.

Families with small children: Offer to seat families with small children in the front row, where they can see and be more engaged in the action of the liturgy. Some parents, however, may prefer to be close to bathrooms, near the cry room, or near an exit so that they'll feel comfortable meeting the needs of their children with little disturbance to the rest of the assembly. Be sure they know how welcome and valued their children are.

People with disabilities: Know which areas are accessible to people in wheelchairs or to those who use canes or walkers. Direct people with hearing disabilities to seating that will enable them to hear as best as they can or to see the sign language interpreter if your parish offers that service. Offer hearing assistance devices if your parish has them. Some people with mental illness experience side effects from medications that cause them to be restless and to pace. Indicate a place they can stand or pace without distracting the congregation or presider while still being able to participate in the liturgy.

Helping people find a seat is an important service that can relieve their stress and make them feel welcome.

Visitors unfamiliar with Catholic worship: If visitors identify themselves as being unfamiliar with Catholic worship, do whatever you can to make them feel comfortable. Give them a worship aid with an Order of Mass so they can follow along and read the responses.

Latecomers: Know what to do with latecomers. Be aware of empty spaces, and help them find places to sit so they can enter into the liturgy as smoothly as possible. Ask your coordinator if there are some points in the liturgy when you should tactfully ask latecomers to wait at the back, and seat them when that moment has passed. Parishes have a variety of policies.

Overflow seating: Know the procedures for overflow seating during busy times. Where can people stand and not impede the action of the liturgy? Does the parish have folding, stacking chairs to provide additional seats? Know where they are stored and where they should be placed if there are no fire restrictions. Is there an overflow space?

During the Liturgy

BE A MODEL OF PARTICIPATION

Working as an usher or a greeter isn't something you just show up to do because it's nice to volunteer and you're friendly. It is part of the liturgy; it is the work of the people of God. Certainly, you are there for others, but you are also there to participate in the liturgy so that you too will be built up, made into a holy temple of the Lord. So you must take your duty to participate in the liturgy as seriously as you take your duties as a minister. They work together like hand in glove.

This means that even though you may need to be at your station to welcome and usher latecomers, you also need to be attentive to and participating in the beginning of the liturgy; you sing the song and voice the responses.

When it is time to take a seat, you join the assembly. Your parish may have reserved seating for you, but you are part of the assembly. Even if your seats are separate from the pews, your postures and actions should indicate that you are still a member of the assembly. Rise when everyone stands, sit when everyone sits, and kneel when everyone kneels unless your role calls you to another position.

Model the appropriate actions. If you need a review, read a current missal or another resource recommended at the end of this book.

Focus your attention on the action of the liturgy. Look at the lector, cantor, deacon, or priest during the proclamation of the Word; look to the presider and the action at the altar during the Liturgy of the Eucharist.

Know and exhibit the proper postures and gestures for the prayers of the liturgy and for receiving Communion.

Sing throughout the liturgy. (God loves your voice, no matter what you think of it!)

> While the liturgy daily builds up those who are within [the Church], into a holy temple of the Lord, into a dwelling place for God in the Spirit, to the mature measure of the fullness of Christ, at the same time it marvelously strengthens their power to preach Christ and thus shows forth the church to those who are outside as a sign lifted up among the nations until there is one sheepfold and one shepherd.
>
> —*Sacrosanctum concilium*, 2

Be attentive to the needs of your fellow ushers and greeters and to those of the other ministers of the liturgy, but don't get involved in unnecessary conversation.

ASSISTING WITH PROCESSIONS AND OTHER DUTIES

Opening Procession: The moments surrounding the opening procession can be busy, even hectic. Ushers and greeters can assist by guiding last-minute arrivals around rather than through the group while they assemble. Direct people to the side doors and up side aisles, so that they don't become tangled in the procession and so the lines of sight and communication between the presider and the musicians remain clear.

Procession for the Liturgy of the Word with Children: If your parish has ministers who celebrate the Liturgy of the Word with children in a separate space, the presider will call them and the children to come forward to assemble after the opening prayer. Find out what your parish expects of you at this time. Do the ushers accompany the procession to the doors? Is there a door that needs to be held open for the children or that needs to be closed after they've left the worship space? Check with your coordinator about the practice at your parish.

Dismissal of Catechumens: When there are people who have been accepted into the Order of Catechumens through the process of the Rite of Christian Initiation of Adults (RCIA), the catechumens may be present at the Mass at which you are serving. Usually they are dismissed from the assembly after the homily so that they may spend time breaking open the Word they have just heard proclaimed. The coordinator of the ushers and greeters should make sure that you know when and how this will happen. Is there a door that needs to be opened or closed after they have left the worship space? Be sure you know where the group goes after the dismissal because after Mass, the friends and families of the catechumens may need directions to find the group.

Return of the Children to the Assembly: Parishes handle the return of the children to the assembly after the Liturgy of the Word in different ways. Most often the children will return as the collection is being taken. The choreography of this event is an issue for the liturgy committee to discuss, and your coordinator should communicate it to you, so that their return can be a joyous reintegration into the community rather than a haphazard flurry of activity.

The Collection: Your coordinator will explain the pattern to follow at your parish and assign the section of the assembly for which you will be responsible. Some parishes use long-handled baskets that the usher extends to all of the people in the pew. If this is what you will be using, practice handling the basket when it is empty and when it is heavy with coins. Be mindful of your movements so that you don't accidentally strike anything or anyone with the long handle. Be attentive to all the people in the row so you don't miss anyone or make anyone who is not contributing feel self-conscious. Try to notice when some-

As you collect peoples' offerings, be sure to wear a friendly face.

one isn't quite ready, and let them know you'll return for their contribution if waiting for them at that moment will delay the collection too long. In other parishes, small baskets are passed down each row, person to person. In that case, be ready to give direction when someone in the pew is confused about which way to pass the basket. As you collect peoples' offerings, be sure to wear a friendly face. Make eye contact, smile, and remember that people are offering the gift of their treasure as well as their hearts in preparation for the next movement of the liturgy.

The Presentation of the Gifts: In the action of carrying to the altar our gifts of bread and wine and money or offerings for the poor, we express our desire to become part of this exchange with God. The members of the assembly who carry our gifts forward represent the entire assembly, so take care to invite a diverse range of ages and ethnicities to participate from week to week. Consider asking family members who are there for the baptism of a child, a couple who may be celebrating an anniversary, a young adult home from school for a holiday, or an engaged couple who will be marrying soon. This procession should not be rushed, and the presentation of our offering of money should be as intentional as our presentation of the bread and wine. In many parishes, the money is acknowledged and received by the presider, even when good stewardship requires that it be taken directly to a secure place for safekeeping.

Communion Procession: Your coordinator will know what is expected. In some parishes the procession flows well and ushers can simply stand out of the way. If your help is needed, be aware of visitors who may not know the routine in your space. Make eye contact and gesture to lead them in the right direction. Most people will be able to follow the lead of the people in front of them, but be particularly mindful on days when the first pews may be full of family and friends joining the assembly for a baptism. It's possible that many of them will not have been to church for a while or may not be Catholic. In that case, they won't be able to "lead" the procession. Take a moment before Mass to let them know the procedures and what to do if they are not going to Communion. This situation may arise on other occasions as well, such as funerals and weddings.

Be aware of people with disabilities who may not be able to join in the procession, and alert the ministers of Communion to come to them. Some people with disabilities will be able, and will want, to join the procession. Don't assume that they want the ministers to come to them. Ask.

Be considerate of the people who want to remain in the pews. Acknowledge their presence; don't overlook them. Let them know when someone needs to move around them.

During celebrations that are especially crowded, such as Christmas and Easter, when there are likely to be visitors unfamiliar with the worship space and the pattern followed for the Communion procession, you may need to be more attentive. Work with your coordinator in advance to plan for extra Communion stations and to work out the movement of the procession. No matter how urgent the need for order, always be gentle and kind as well as firm.

As the Assembly Is Sent Forth

RETURN TO YOUR STATION

During the closing song, move to your station (most likely the location where you did your welcoming as people assembled).

Someone Should Assist the Ministers in the Recessional

One of the ushers or greeters should be responsible for attending to the needs of the ministers who are part of the recessional. Take their songbooks; make sure the altar servers extinguish their candles, and help them make their way through the crowds, so that fire and hot wax don't become a problem.

Saying Goodbye and Distributing the Parish Bulletin

When saying goodbye, share Christ's love and peace, keeping your attention on the people.

In the same way that you made the effort to greet everyone upon arrival and made him or her feel welcome, now you will take the time to reinforce the message of the dismissal, "Go in peace, glorifying the Lord by your life." Do your best to ensure that everyone receives a copy of the parish bulletin and an acknowledgment of his or her participation in the day's celebration: smile and encourage each person to come back again. Make this moment a moment of sharing Christ's love and peace, keeping your attention on the people.

The bulletin is full of news and information on the many ways in which we are Church. This is where the people read about forthcoming weddings and baptisms, read the names of members who have recently died, and read the names of those who have recently become new members of the parish. They learn about the children preparing to celebrate the sacraments. This is where the dates and times of the meetings of all the ministries are posted. The bulletin is part of the glue that holds the community together, so it's important that everyone receives a copy.

Events after the Liturgy

When there are special events after the liturgy, direct people to the next event. Don't lead the group to it, though; remain at your station to direct others and to say goodbye to people who aren't staying.

Caring for the Collection

If the collection wasn't moved to a secure place during the liturgy, this is the time for the designated ushers to make sure that it is guarded and taken to the appropriate place. Every parish should have procedures for this. You need to follow them to the letter.

After the Liturgy

Once the assembly has dispersed, it's time to deal with the practicalities of cleaning up. Check for lost items, return hymnals to their proper places.

Collect disposable worship aids to be recycled. Pick up trash. Remove reserved signs that won't be needed for the next liturgy. Take off your usher or greeter tag and put it away so that the ministers of the next liturgy can find it.

Depending on the timing between Masses, the ushers and greeters for the next liturgy may be arriving. Greet them. Let them know about any special events or actions that will take place, and make them aware of any problems that might have arisen or might reoccur. If someone left something valuable, let the next ushers and greeters know where to find it, in case the owner comes looking for it during the next liturgy.

Special Circumstances

Dealing with Distractions

Distractions, although they can draw one's attention, are generally harmless and do not interfere with the Eucharistic celebration. Often no intervention is needed beyond casting a concerned look in their direction.

RESTLESS CHILDREN

A restless or crying child isn't an annoyance; he or she is one of the members of the Body of Christ. Check with your coordinator about the practices of your parish. Some parishes occasionally put notices in the bulletin to reassure parents that children are welcome in the assembly and a certain amount of restlessness and noise is expected. Let them know what resources might be available to help (a cry room or adjacent area where parents can take children who need attention). When children are noisy, it might feel intrusive to the parent for an usher or greeter to approach the pew and offer assistance. But when the parent is bringing an unhappy child to the back of the church, it is hospitable to meet the parent there with a sympathetic word and offer of help.

CELL PHONES

Most people appreciate being reminded to silence their cell phones—either through signage as they enter the church, in a note on the worship aid, or in an announcement before Mass begins. No one wants to cause that sort of distraction—and yet it happens. Unless for some reason a ringing phone is left untended in a pew with no one to take care of it, this situation does not need attention from a hospitality minister.

Dealing with Disruptions

Disruptions are more serious than distractions. They interfere with the celebration of the liturgy, can be frightening, could put people in danger, and will require some sort of intervention.

Aggressive Behavior

As a result of intoxication, untreated mental illness, or significant developmental disability, people can display aggressive behavior. This might include shouting loudly, making threatening gestures, or intruding into the personal space of others. Often the best intervention is simply to observe from a distance; the behavior may be short-lived, and the problem might resolve on its own. At times, you might want to position yourself closer to the person to let them know you are concerned, keeping another hospitality minister in your line of sight in case you need to summon help.

Behavioral Emergencies

When someone is threatening physical harm to themselves or others, or will not stop their disruptive behavior, you can consider the situation a behavioral emergency. Like all emergencies, experts in emergency response need to be summoned. It can be useful for you to know ahead of time who in the parish is a mental health professional or has worked in law enforcement or the military. These people can be invaluable resources in an emergency if you ask them to assist you. They may have more expert skills in engaging the person and bringing about a safe resolution of the emergency. However, when the situation cannot be resolved safely with parish resources, outside help needs to be called in. When calling 911 or another local emergency number, provide a clear description of the behavior, the best door to enter, and whether a medical response will be needed in addition to law enforcement. Depending upon your location, a special crisis response team consisting of law enforcement officers and mental health professionals may be dispatched. When these responders arrive, answer their questions succinctly and objectively, and then follow their directions.

Medical Emergencies

Here's where that first-aid course may come in handy. You'll be much more likely to respond quickly if you know what to do. But if you don't have any first-aid training, don't let that keep you from doing something. If you know of medical professionals in the assembly, alert them. Know where the first-aid kit is. Keep your cell phone with you during Mass (though silenced, of course) so that you can quickly call 911 if necessary. Recognize your limitations; do not try to handle a situation that is beyond your capabilities.

As to whether the liturgy should be halted until an emergency situation (behavioral, medical, or of any sort) is resolved, the presider will make that judgment. Ministers of hospitality try to balance the need to preserve order and quiet so that the liturgy is not disrupted with the paramount concern of charity—caring for an individual in crisis. By all means, life-saving efforts must proceed as quickly as possible. The presider will decide whether medical or emergency personnel can do their work in the background, or whether the situation is so dire that liturgical action should stop and silent prayer for the sufferer should ensue until needs are met.

Natural Disasters

Know the procedures to deal with situations that are likely in your region of the country. Do you live in a place where tornadoes, hurricanes, or earthquakes are possibilities? Where are the safe places in your church building? What is the plan for evacuation, if necessary, and for uniting children who may be in religious education classes with parents who might be in the church?

Fire

Every building should have a plan for evacuation in case of fire. Know where all the exits are. Know where all the fire extinguishers are and how to use them. This is another circumstance where you should not try to handle a situation that is beyond your capabilities.

Violence

Many churches and parish schools have developed procedures to follow in case of a violent act or the threat of one. If your parish has not done this, raise it with your coordinator. Violence may erupt from circumstances such as racial, ethnic, or religious hatred, gangs, quarrels among family or friends, or mental illness.

In some security plans, the greeters' direct eye contact and verbal interaction with those entering the church is considered to be both a heartfelt expression of caring and a sort of threat assessment. But it's important not to misinterpret unusual behavior as a threat when it may simply be the result of harmless personality quirks or mental illness.

All of these emergency situations require carefully considered and clearly communicated procedures. If your parish has not informed you of them, approach your coordinator so that these issues can be addressed.

Special Liturgies and Occasions

Solemnities, Feasts, and Memorials

Some of these special days in our liturgical calendar will call for changes in the actions of the liturgy. Sprinkling rites, special processions, the use of incense—all of these things should be communicated to you through your coordinator. There are several books that give guidelines and suggestions for celebrating the liturgies of the year. All liturgical ministers should have access to one of them through their coordinator. For example, *Sourcebook for Sundays, Seasons, and Weekdays: The Almanac for Pastoral Liturgy* (Liturgy Training Publications) addresses the issues in every season and for every day of the liturgical year. It can help you know in advance what special actions you should be prepared to facilitate. However, your coordinator will inform you about the specific way your parish will celebrate on a certain day.

Baptism, First Communion, and Confirmation: Your parish may celebrate these sacraments of initiation for infants, children, and teens within the context of Sunday Mass. Even when they are not celebrated during a Sunday liturgy, they are still parish celebrations, and ideally, ushers and greeters will be scheduled. Such liturgies are special opportunities to welcome the families and friends of these children. For many, this may be the first time in a while that they have been in church, and your presence can help to make the experience joyful. These are moments for evangelization, when the hearts of those who have been inactive can be touched by a loving and warm parish community.

Weddings and Funerals: Often these liturgies are attended primarily by family and friends, but they are parish celebrations too, and ushers and greeters should be scheduled. The specific needs of the people who gather for weddings are very different from those of the people gathering for funerals, but both groups need to be welcomed and put at ease.

Wedding celebrations call people together in joy, but they are often stressful days for the bride and groom, the wedding party, and the immediate family. Usually, friends or family of the couple will be ushers, seating the guests and distributing the worship aids, but a few veteran greeters who know where things are and can answer guests' questions will help things run smoothly.

When people gather for a funeral, the feelings of loss and sadness make the necessity for compassionate ministers of hospitality even more important. In your parish, there may be a special bereavement ministry that provides ushers and greeters for funeral liturgies. If not, work with your coordinator, the liturgy director, pastoral associate, deacon, or pastor to learn about any special procedures.

Other Types of Liturgies—Liturgy of the Hours, Liturgies of the Word, and Devotions: Parishes gather to worship and celebrate in many ways beyond Sunday Mass, the other sacraments, and funerals. These may include Morning Prayer or Evening Prayer, a Liturgy of the Word, Penance Services, Stations of the Cross, recitations of the Rosary, adoration and benediction of the Blessed Sacrament. Ushers and greeters may be scheduled. Your duties wouldn't be identical to those at Sunday Mass, but the primary responsibility for hospitality remains. You would be attentive to the needs of the gathered community, making them feel welcome, safe, and comfortable. You might distribute worship aids, and as always, you would model heartfelt participation. There may be different kinds of processions to facilitate, and perhaps more people will be unfamiliar with the actions and movements. When you are scheduled to be part of a service that is new to you, be sure to get in touch with your coordinator to learn more about your duties. Ask questions about the service, too, so that you'll understand your role as a prayerful participant.

Being a Responsible Member of the Ministry Team

Be dependable! Show up every time you are scheduled to minister. The role of the hospitality minister is just as important and vital to the life of the parish as every other minister's role. After all, you are the first face people will associate with the Church when they arrive. If you can't make your scheduled Mass, follow the procedures to find a replacement. Keep the schedule close at hand. Mark your scheduled days in your date book or on your calendar. Let the coordinator know when you're available and when you're not. If situations in your life change, making it difficult to keep your commitment to the ministry, talk to your coordinator and take time off from the ministry until you can make a new commitment.

Be willing to learn. Reading this guide is a good start. Turn to the Resources section and plan to do some of the additional reading as well.

Continue to grow spiritually. Participate in the formation sessions that your parish offers for its liturgical ministers. Grow as a person of the Word and a person of prayer.

Be an active member of the parish. You are welcoming people into the life of the Church. How can you welcome people into this life if you are not living it too? No one can join everything or participate in every event, but make the effort to participate in at least some catechetical, service, and social events. When your parish hosts hospitality times after masses or for special occasions, and you are scheduled to greet, go—not just because you have agreed to do so but because you like people. The more connections you make with people outside of Sunday Mass, the more connected they will feel when you greet them at the door.

Questions for Reflection and Discussion

1. What information and skills do you need to learn in order to be an effective minister of hospitality? How are you going to learn them?

2. Which of the tasks in this ministry will be the easiest and most natural for you?

3. Which tasks seem like they might be difficult for you?

4. What approaches to the different tasks in this ministry have you observed to be especially effective?

5. Whom could you ask to mentor you in this new ministry until you feel confident?

Chapter Four

Spirituality and Discipleship

*The love of God has been poured out into our hearts
through the holy Spirit that has been given to us.*

—Romans 5:5

Ministers of hospitality have tasks to accomplish. They greet worshippers at the door. They help people find a place. They take up the collection. But these are not merely tasks on a checklist. They are ministries. And they require a minister's heart, full of love.

The attitude you bring to your role is as important as the work you do. You perform this ministry at church. Your faith is its primary motivation. You believe in God. You love God. You want to serve God with the love you have received. You express your desire to serve in a variety of ways, and being a minister of hospitality is one of them. You show the quality of your love for God in the way you greet people, tend to their needs, handle their money, and answer their questions.

It is hard to be like Christ all the time. But especially when we are at church, the power of his sacrifice summons us to share his spirit of service with others and to let the charity of the Holy Spirit flow through us.

Some people are harder to welcome than others. But the doors of our churches are wide open. Christ welcomes even the stranger and the sinner so that all may be transformed.

An improper welcome has its consequences. When Jesus sent the Twelve out in pairs, he knew that some people would reject the message he asked the disciples to preach. "Whatever place does not welcome you or listen to you, leave there and shake the dust off your feet in testimony against them."[1] You have entered some places where you did not feel welcome. And you have probably promised yourself you'd never go back. This can happen to some who attend your church. But you can help them have a positive experience of the building and its people.

After Mass and throughout the week, strive to cultivate a hospitable heart. Work on the demeanor that you will bring with you to church. This works both ways. Your service at church will also help you keep a kindly spirit at home and at work throughout the next week.

---

1. Mark 6:11.

Be Welcoming

Some people have a natural gift for hospitality. They love the company of others. They brighten up when you enter the room. They want you to visit their residence, and they give you their full attention when you do. They want you to be at home—literally: *"Mi casa, su casa."*

Other people put these skills into play at work. Especially if their job is to sell products, they have learned the value of being friendly and building trust with customers. You are more likely to buy from someone who has earned your trust. In many businesses, sales bring commissions, so being a friendly sales representative brings financial rewards. Good salespeople don't put on an act. They sincerely believe in their product and sincerely want to help you.

Some places of business hire people to greet customers at the door. From grocery stores to concert halls, when you enter the building, you may come face to face with a volunteer wearing a name badge, a smock, and a smile. The company doesn't expect them to make the sale, just to make others welcome. These volunteers are often some of the most informed people around. They can answer basic questions about your needs, and they do it politely. Good greeters don't force themselves on you. If you don't need their assistance, their act of hospitality is to smile and let you pass, respectful of the knowledge and intent you bring along.

Greeters at church use these same skills. The difference between them and business greeters is the reason they are there. At places of business, the greeter is on duty because of a belief in the business. At church, the greeter is on duty because of a belief in God. The opportunity to share faith endows each encounter at church with deeper meaning than one can obtain from locating the proper aisle for canned fruit.

You greet people all day long. You do it on the phone, through email, texting, and in person. Think for a moment about the communications you've made in the past few days, whether at home or at work, doing chores or resting up.

- How did you react when the phone rang? Did you feel inconvenienced? Was it noticeable in your voice?
- How do you handle telemarketers? Do you hang up on them? Do you refuse to listen to them? Do you get angry? Do you politely turn them aside?
- How do you respond to email? Are you quick and accurate? Do you ever respond with rage to an online message?
- How do you respond when a stranger asks for help? Are you anxious to be of service, or anxious to get away?
- Do you judge by appearances? When the person asking you for help has a different color skin than you do, a different accent than your friends use,

or different clothes than you wear, do you find yourself getting tense? Do you avoid persons of a certain age—young or old? Are you more likely to help the handsome and the beautiful than the sick and disfigured?

When you greet people at church, you are greeting each one as a child of God. You greet them not as a potential client, not as an inconvenience, but as another member of the Body of Christ.

If you want to learn the names of people at church, develop the skill. Learn the names of your neighbors and coworkers.

To be a good host, be a good guest. When someone feeds you dinner, send them a note of thanks. They have done you a favor. They have helped you be a better greeter. After friends welcome you as a guest—whether or not they make a good impression—you understand better how to welcome others.

Jesus emphasized the importance of giving welcome. He knew that those who were not welcomed might feel excluded. So he taught his followers to include others, especially those they might have preferred to avoid.

For a better understanding of the roots of Christian hospitality, look up the passages listed below in your Bible.

1. **Matthew 18:5.** When the disciples tried to keep children from pestering Jesus, he thought their opinion was completely misguided: "Whoever receives one child such as this in my name receives me."[2]

2. **Luke 15:20.** In the parable of the prodigal son, the father had every reason to be angry with his son. But when the son returns from his sinful escapade, the father runs out to meet him. He loves the son so much that he sees the needy person behind the greedy person.

3. **Luke 15:2.** Jesus perplexed the Pharisees with his habit of dining with sinners. It scandalized those who thought they were religious, but Jesus obviously felt it was the proper thing to do.

After the death of Jesus, the disciples hungered for a hearty welcome. They were undergoing persecution, so the embrace of friendship meant a lot to them.

1. **Romans 16:2.** Paul asks the church at Rome to give Phoebe a welcome fitting for saints.

2. **Colossians 4:10.** Paul wasn't sure whether Mark would be able to visit the Church at Colossae, but he sent this message to the members there: "If he comes to you, receive him."

3. **2 Corinthians 7:15.** Paul compliments the Church at Corinth for the way they welcomed Titus. Titus was so impressed that he had told Paul

---

2. See also Mark 9:37 and Luke 9:48.

about it, and Paul was so impressed he acknowledged the kindness of that Church.

4. **Acts 15:4 and 21:7–8. Galatians 4:14.** These three passages all indicate the kind of welcome Paul received on different occasions. They show how much the early Church prized the virtue of hospitality.

5. **Acts 28:30.** Paul was kept under guard for two years in Rome, but he welcomed all who came to him.

A good way to cultivate a hospitable heart is to be welcoming to everyone —saint and sinner—whether at work, at home, or at church.

Discern Needs

Be attentive to the needs of those who come to church. You can also practice this skill all week long. When you enter a place of business just in front of someone else, hold the door open. When someone needs help carrying groceries, lend a hand. When parents seem stressed with the needs of their children, offer a smile and a word of encouragement. When a child is alone or in some potential danger, get help.

All of these are everyday skills. Responding with compassion to those in need is a basic human virtue. Even those who do not profess faith in Christ help other human beings, and their actions fill them with satisfaction.

Human hospitality is sanctioned and sanctified by Christ. Evidence for this appears throughout the Gospel, but these passages will give you much food for thought:

1. **Matthew 25:31–46.** Jesus imagines a king who separates people as a shepherd separates sheep from goats. He praises those who fed the hungry, gave drink to the thirsty, welcomed the stranger, clothed the naked, cared for the sick, and visited the prisoner. When do you perform these actions in your life? Are you aware that you are doing these things for Christ?

2. **Luke 9:11.** When the crowds followed Jesus, he was anxious to take care of their needs. He even provided food in abundance from a few loaves and fish. Everyone knows the story of the miracle of the loaves, but St. Luke's account includes one especially lovely detail. Before Jesus started teaching, before it became evening, and before the Twelve faced a food and housing problem of immense proportions, Jesus did something else. His first action for these people, according to Luke, was this: "He received them."

People are coming to church hungry for the bread of life and the cup of salvation. Nothing will feed them like the Eucharist. But something else happens before they begin to worship: You receive them. You sense their physical and spiritual needs.

How will you do this? As you get to know them, practice their names, and learn about their lives, you will be better able to hear their sorrows and to offer your prayer and support.

Some of the needs you discern are spiritually deep. People are looking for a way to live a better life, not just to worship. Sometimes all they need is a welcome, some human contact, some attention that says they are worth something. With that can come a complete change in behavior.

Have you ever been so welcomed someplace that it changed your outlook? Have you ever been so impressed by someone's faith and love that you wanted to improve your behavior to be worthy of the friendship? How will you present yourself to churchgoers this weekend?

Be Prudent and Trustworthy

When you collect the offering, you are receiving a gift that people hold precious and transferring it to an organization that represents their deepest values. The collection also symbolizes the gift of each person at the altar with Christ. The collection is serious business.

How do you handle money in your own life? Are you a good steward of it? Are you generous to those in need?

The concept of stewardship teaches that none of us really owns anything. The possessions we have and the money in our accounts aren't really ours. They are God's. God made everything, and God owns everything. God has placed certain things in our care. We are stewards of what God owns.

How are you doing as a steward? If you consider that the money in your accounts is not really yours, that it is God's, are you responsibly handling God's money? How do you spend it? Are you keeping more than you need while others struggle to make ends meet? Are you contributing faithfully to your parish, to your diocese, and to other charities? What types of businesses and entertainments do you support? How much excess do you already own? If you rendered an account of your stewardship, what would God see?

How are you managing your personal debts? Do you spend more than you have? Are you a responsible steward?

When you take up the collection, you are taking up God's collection. If you have a habit of contributing generously, you will understand the sacrifice and charity that lie behind these simple gifts.

Strive to live as a person worthy of trust. When you stand in front of people with a basket in your hands, you are asking them to trust you with their offering. All through the week—not just on Sunday—practice the virtue of honesty. Do you tell the truth? Can people trust you with their secrets? Do you avoid gossip and slander? Do people trust you to watch their children, their homes, their purse? If so, you have one of the qualities it takes to be a good usher, greeter, or minister of hospitality.

Consider Luke 19:6. Zacchaeus was too short to see Jesus above the heads of the crowd, so he climbed a sycamore tree for a better view. No one exercised hospitality toward Zacchaeus. Anyone could have made way for him, could have let him stand in front, or could have helped him aloft. But no one did. When Jesus spots Zacchaeus, the conversation he has with him reveals some aspects of hospitality. Jesus invites *himself* over to stay at Zacchaeus' house. And Zacchaeus happily issues a welcome. Then Zacchaeus does something more. He has a reputation as a sinner, and he wants to overcome this. He tells Jesus he will give half of his possessions to the poor and pay back any fraudulent activity fourfold. All this because Jesus invited himself over!

Being a giver can change your personality. Once you start giving, you think less of yourself and more of others. You make amends for the irresponsible financial decisions of your past, and for trying to justify keeping to yourself what rightfully belongs to others. Before you collect money from other donors at church, have you scrutinized your own financial habits?

Be Knowledgeable about the Parish

Get to know your parish on a deep level, and be ready to share that knowledge with others. When you stand in the narthex or vestibule of your church, some people will ask you for information. When you pass out bulletins at the end of the service, people naturally presume you know what's in them. Good ministers of hospitality have more than surface knowledge. They know the heart and spirit of their parish because they have been participating in its life.

Are you participating in parish activities? Is Sunday Mass a priority each week? When adult education is offered, do you take part? Do you come for the seasonal penance services? Have you helped with the religious formation of children? How have you volunteered to be of service to the Body of Christ at nursing homes, prisons, or hospitals? When you take an active role in parish life, you will be more deeply informed about your church, able to convincingly encourage fellow parishioners to participate, and you will be a better model for others who come to worship.

In Luke 9:13, Jesus tells a parable about two men who go to the temple to pray. One stands, looks up to heaven, and proclaims that he is not like sinners. He fasts, prays, and tithes. But he also boasts. The other man stands far off, beats his breast, turns his gaze down, and asks God to have mercy on him, a sinner.

Which are you? Are you the one who boasts about your spiritual accomplishments? Are you a haughty volunteer? Or are you the one who comes to church humble, aware of your sins, knowing that you need God's mercy to live a faithful life?

Be Part of the Team

When you serve as an usher or greeter in your parish, you are part of a team of people offering their service to God. Welcome one another, as you welcome others.

Hospitality is truly everyone's job. Everybody coming to church deserves a welcome, and this shouldn't fall to you alone to do the work. Still, you are part of a team that specializes in welcoming. You have given hospitality a lot of thought and prayer, and you will model this for the rest of the parish.

Be friendly toward the other ministers of hospitality. You do not own any turf here; you are all working together. Your sincere love for one another will center your ministry.

You will need the assistance of other people—you cannot perform this ministry alone. Worshippers will want to see you, but they may be happy to see another usher or greeter, too. This is a team activity. The faithful should be able to find the face of Christ among the ministers of hospitality.

Nonetheless, avoid being so focused on other ushers and greeters that you neglect your duty toward those entering the building. Some greeters spend so much time greeting one another, or the reader, or the priest, that they miss seeing many people who enter and leave the church. Your camaraderie with other ministers is a good foundation, but it should move you into your mission of hospitality to others.

How do you work at hospitality at home? Is it the work of everyone who lives there? Or does someone else have the responsibility of making people feel at home? How do you use other members of your household to widen the welcome mat?

At family gatherings, are you a good host and a good guest? Are there some people you try to avoid? Do you build community with everyone? Does forgiveness need to happen? Is there something you can do? Are you able to help someone in the family who feels estranged?

Be Prayerful

In Luke 10:40 we find perhaps the most famous story of hospitality in the Gospels—Jesus' visit to the home of Martha. It is a puzzling story, and well worth your meditation.

In a certain village, Jesus visited the home of Martha, and she welcomed him there. Her sister Mary sat at Jesus' feet and listened to him. But Martha was busy with the tasks of hospitality. Martha was getting a little annoyed that Mary just sat there when so much work needed to be done. Martha did not expect Jesus to help; after all, he was a guest. But Mary was her sister, and she should have known better.

All this seems very reasonable, even today. Having someone over to your house is work. You want the house to be clean, you have shopped and have prepared the food and drinks, and you know there'll be plenty to clean up when the visit is over. If you do it by yourself, it's a lot of work. It's good to have a little assistance.

So, what Martha was asking does not seem out of line. She's busy, and Mary could have made this a lot easier if she had just gotten off the floor and helped out.

But Jesus scolds *Martha*. He sees something else. He sees that Martha is worried and distracted. Mary is the one who is focused. Mary sees what is important about this visit. Jesus is there. The Word of God is living, active, and resting in the living room. Martha was busy for the sake of being busy. She was avoiding the words of Jesus. Jesus certainly had important things to say to her, things that could have helped lower her anxiety and eased her worry. But Martha was not ready for that word. She busied herself and avoided the hard task of listening to Jesus and changing her life.

Be prayerful and attentive to God's presence—at Mass and at all times.

As a hospitality minister, you have work to do. Making people feel at home at church is not easy. It requires a lot of time and attention. Your work is important to the whole church.

But something else is even more important: the time you take with Jesus. Your ministry to the church is admirable. Keep it up! But your prayer is also necessary. Don't let it slip!

Throughout the course of the week, spend time listening to the Words of Jesus, as Mary did in Martha's home. Put down the other tasks of your life, and spend time with Jesus, who is our Lord and friend.

Read over the Sunday Scripture readings before you come to church. You are in a vulnerable position. Latecomers may need your attention when the reader is proclaiming the Word of God. If you have spent time with the readings before coming to church, you will be more able to hear them as they are proclaimed.

When you are at church, pray the Mass. Once the Mass begins, and especially during the Liturgy of the Word, God is speaking to the Church. Jesus is speaking in the Gospel. Nothing is more important. Yet throughout the Mass many hospitality ministers may be imitating Martha, who was distracted and worried about other things. Remember, Jesus points us toward Mary, who dropped everything when he dropped in. You only get one chance a week to hear the proclamation of the Word of God in the presence of the Church. Do it. Except for emergencies, everything else can wait for just that few moments. If you are going to be a good greeter, first be greeted by the Word of God.

Sing the songs. Make the responses. Listen attentively. Observe the silences. Yes, you have a ministry to perform, but your aim is to learn the art of both attending to the assembly's needs and staying engaged with the holy event of the liturgy that is unfolding before you. Jesus will fill your soul with wisdom, peace, and love.

Prayers for Ushers and Greeters

Prayers you may find helpful are offered here and at the end of the book.

Psalm 131:2

> . . . I have stilled my soul,
> Like a weaned child to its mother,
>   weaned is my soul.

From the Book of Blessings

The Book of Blessings provides a blessing for liturgical ministers, including ushers—from which we can infer all ministers of hospitality. You can find strength and inspiration in the community's prayers for you.

> *For the Church of Christ and for this parish of N., that all Christians*
>   *may offer* themselves as living sacrifices, we pray to the Lord.
> For all the liturgical ministers of our parish, that they may deepen their
> commitment to serve God and their neighbor, we pray to
>   the Lord . . . .
> For these ushers, that their presence may make all who enter this
>   church always feel
> welcome in God's house, we pray to the Lord.
> God of glory,
> your beloved Son has shown us
> that true worship comes from humble and contrite hearts.
>
> Bless our brothers and sisters,
> who have responded to the needs of our parish
> and wish to commit themselves to your service as ushers.
> Grant that their ministry may be fruitful
> and our worship pleasing in your sight.
> We ask this through Christ our Lord.
> Amen.[3]

---

3. BB, 1853–1854.

Also in the *Book of Blessings*, the Church suggests a particular reading from Scripture for the blessing of a new usher. It's a very popular text, one that you hear a great deal at weddings. It may surprise you to find that it is recommended for ushers (and by extension, all ministers of hospitality). It reminds us that the challenge to love is not limited to those you like. It extends to everyone.

1 Corinthians 13:1–13

> If I speak in human and angelic tongues but do not have love, I am a resounding gong or a clashing cymbal. And if I have the gift of prophecy and comprehend all mysteries and all knowledge; if I have all faith so as to move mountains but do not have love, I am nothing. If I give away everything I own, and if I hand my body over so that I may boast but do not have love, I gain nothing.
>
> Love is patient, love is kind. It is not jealous, love is not pompous, it is not inflated, it is not rude, it does not seek its own interests, it is not quick-tempered, it does not brood over injury, it does not rejoice over wrongdoing but rejoices with the truth. It bears all things, believes all things, hopes all things, endures all things.
>
> Love never fails. If there are prophecies, they will be brought to nothing; if tongues, they will cease; if knowledge, it will be brought to nothing. For we know partially and we prophesy partially, but when the perfect comes, the partial will pass away. When I was a child, I used to talk as a child, think as a child, reason as a child; when I became a man, I put aside childish things. At present we see indistinctly, as in a mirror, but then face to face. At present I know partially; then I shall know fully, as I am fully known. So faith, hope, love remain, these three; but the greatest of these is love.[4]

Questions for Reflection and Discussion

1. In my daily life, how could I be more hospitable? Could I be more forgiving, more inviting to members of my family, coworkers, or neighbors?

2. In my daily life, how can I be a better steward? Am I generous enough to those in need? Do I need to change my habits of saving and spending?

3. At church, how can I better be the face of Christ to those who come? It is Jesus who welcomes the Church to his table. How do I assist him?

4. Whom do I love with the love St. Paul describes? Am I stingy with that love? Could I be showing it more gracefully to others? How can I become more discerning about who needs my love, my attention, my care?

---

4. BB, 1863 (1 Corinthians 13:1–13).

Chapter Five

Frequently Asked Questions

1. What's the difference between an usher, a greeter, and a minister of hospitality?

There may not be any difference at all. Some parishes use only one term, either *usher* or *greeter*, and the role description might encompass all or most of the duties and responsibilities described in this book. Other parishes might use both terms to describe two complimentary roles—*greeters* who greet the members of the assembly as they gather, and *ushers* who handle seating, assist in the processions, take up the collection, and are ready to help with emergencies. Still other parishes may not make a distinction, but give everyone the title *minister of hospitality*. Whatever specific role you are trained for, you are a minister of hospitality.

2. What are the qualities needed for this ministry?

Ushers and greeters should be people who are already coming to worship regularly. They should be mature, confirmed Catholics in whom the pastor feels confident placing his trust. They should express a genuine love for people, be comfortable in large groups, have excellent people skills, and be responsible and dependable. Young people can be fine ministers of hospitality—especially greeting—and could be mentored in those aspects of the ministry that call for experienced judgment. Children often enjoy serving with their parents.

3. How will I know when to begin the collection of offerings?

The collection of offerings takes place after the universal prayer (or prayer of the faithful). Usually when the priest finishes the concluding prayer after the intentions, the ministers come forward with their baskets to begin the collection. Your coordinator will tell you just when you should begin moving from your seat to the place where the baskets have been set out so that you will be ready for this moment. This is one of the times you may have to move around the church while another liturgical action is taking place. Be sure to do it as unobtrusively as possible.

4. If there is a second collection, how will I know when to begin?

Parishes arrange second collections in different ways. Your coordinator will advise you.

5. What should I do if I run out of bulletins?

Find out ahead of time from your coordinator where extras might be kept—perhaps in the sacristy or church office. You could ask hospitality ministers at other stations if they have extras. If none can be found, apologize graciously, and explain that the bulletin can be found on the parish website, or give the person the phone number of the church office so they can call for any specific information they might need. Be sure to let your coordinator know that you ran out so that more can be printed in the future.

6. What should I do if I'm told that the restrooms have no paper towels or toilet paper?

You will need to know where these supplies are kept so that you can replenish the restrooms. If you don't know, usually someone in the sacristy will know.

7. Some people have favorite places to sit and won't move to let someone else into the pew. How can I persuade people to move or to fill up the pews in the front of the church?

It's true that people can be very set in their ways and attached to a particular place in the church. When there is space available in the middle of the pew and someone is looking for a place to sit, it will be your job to assist them. Most often a simple request will work, "May this gentleman (lady, young woman, family) join you this morning? If the person seems unwilling to move in order to let the others pass by them, a second request could be, "Would you please let these people move past you to their seats? Perhaps you could move out of the pew for just a moment so that they can enter and then you can return to your place."

Encouraging people to fill in the front pews is usually not an easy task. Some people are just shy and feel uncomfortable walking all the way down the aisles, especially if they've arrived late. Accompanying them to the available spaces may be all that's necessary. But maybe they'd truly prefer to stand in the back. Encourage people to take seats in the front, before they become the last available seats. The front row is a great place for families with children—it can be easier to help children to engage in the liturgy if they can see the face of the presider and readers and watch the actions of the liturgy. Just remember that we meet people where they are, and some people will always stay in the back rows. That's okay.

8. When I'm collecting offerings, what should I do if a person is still writing a check or fumbling through a purse or pockets when I come to the row? Should I wait?

You could wait for a few seconds, but if it will clearly be some time before the person is ready, you could tell him or her to bring it to you at the end of Mass and you'll see that it gets into the basket. Your coordinator may have another suggestion.

9. Sometimes, especially at Christmas and Easter, there are so many people that we run out of seats, and crowds are standing in aisles and at the back of the church. They look so uncomfortable. Also, I worry about how we would evacuate the building in the event of an emergency.

These are difficult situations. You will need to ask your coordinator whether there are folding chairs available somewhere and where they can be placed, what the fire codes say about people standing in aisles, and whether the parish might provide overflow seating somewhere else. The parish should be prepared with policies to deal with these situations.

10. What should I do if someone has a medical emergency?

Your parish may already have determined the most efficient way of handling medical emergencies, and your coordinator will give you instructions. At the least, carry your (silenced) cell phone with you during Mass so that you can call for emergency services. If you don't have a cell phone with you, you should know where the nearest phone is and how to call an emergency number. Also, it would be helpful to know if regulars attending the Mass at which you serve are medical professionals who could be of help.

11. Is there anything I should do about cell phones and pagers going off during the Mass?

Your coordinator will tell you how the parish wants to handle this problem. Some parishes make an announcement before the beginning of Mass, asking people to silence their cell phones and pagers. Others put a note in the worship aid or place a sign at the entrance to the worship space.

12. What should I do if a person comes into the building asking assembly members for money?

Of course, everyone is welcome at worship, and you would never turn away someone because of appearances. If a person comes to our doors in need, we are bound to direct them to where they can be helped. However, panhandling in church is not appropriate. Firmly, but gently, ask the person to come to a place where you can talk, find out what is needed, and explain where help can be found. Your coordinator may have more specific guidelines for you to follow. Perhaps your pastor or deacon would want to speak to the person after Mass to learn more about their needs.

13. What if incense sets off a fire alarm in the church during the liturgy?

Raise this possibility with your coordinator so that you can find out what your parish would want done. Someone should be designated to turn off the fire alarm and to reassure people that there is no emergency. But it will be important to be sure the incense is the culprit and not some other actual fire danger.

14. What should I do if an animal comes into the church—a dog, cat, bird, bat, or other creature?

If this occurs before or after Mass, you could try to coax or herd the animal out with the help of others, being careful not to frighten or antagonize it. If the entry occurs during the Mass, you obviously wouldn't want to cause a disruption. If you can't address the problem easily and unobtrusively, wait until the end of Mass. Flying creatures are especially challenging. Aside from opening doors and windows to allow an avenue of exit, there may be nothing you can do until the crowds have left the building.

Resources

Documents and Resources Related to the Liturgy

Sacrosanctum concilium.

> The first document of the Second Vatican Council, promulgated on December 4, 1963, also known by its English title, *Constitution on the Sacred Liturgy*. It allowed the celebration of liturgical rites in the vernacular, called for the full, conscious, and active participation of the assembly, and ordered the revision of all liturgical rites.

General Instruction of the Roman Missal.

> The introductory document, or praenotanda, that explains the theological background and gives the directions for celebrating the Mass. It appears at the beginning of *The Roman Missal* and is published separately.

Sourcebook for Sundays, Seasons, and Weekdays: The Almanac for Pastoral Liturgy. Chicago: Liturgy Training Publications, published annually.

> This resource will take you day by day through the liturgical year, describing the ritual actions, readings, and preparations needed for each liturgy.

Laughlin, Corinna. *The Liturgy: The Source and Summit of Our Christian Life.* Chicago: Liturgy Training Publications, 2018.

> This inviting little book is the best place to begin when learning about the liturgy—the most important thing Catholic Christians do. We learn that liturgy is an encounter with Christ, a marvelous exchange between God and humanity, and a school of faith. Finally, we learn that the liturgy sends us into the world with a mission.

Driscoll, Jeremy, OSB. *What Happens at Mass, Revised Edition.* Chicago: Liturgy Training Publications, 2005.

> This spiritual tour of the Mass by a Benedictine abbot and esteemed teacher of liturgy is engaging and simply written. It will provide insights for every reader interested in the liturgy.

Huck, Gabe. *Liturgy with Style and Grace, Third Edition, Revised.* Chicago: Liturgy Training Publications, 2018.

> This revised classic offers a wide range of liturgical information in a series of two-page articles about the elements of our worship: words and music, Scripture and tradition, symbols and seasons, people and places—including liturgical ministers.

Coffey, Kathy, Donna M. Crilly, et al. *Companion to the Calendar: A Guide to the Saints, Seasons, and Holidays of the Year.* Second Edition. Chicago: Liturgy Training Publications, 2012.

> This book is a lively introduction to the liturgical year—its seasons, solemnities, feasts, memorials, and many other holidays as well.

Pastoral Liturgy®. Chicago: Liturgy Training Publications, published bimonthly.

This bimonthly magazine, vividly illustrated with photos of parish liturgical life, provides articles that deepen appreciation and understanding of parish liturgy for everyone involved in it—especially liturgical ministers. For highlights, visit http://pastoralliturgy.org/.

Resources for Prayer and Spirituality

At Home with the Word®: *Sunday Scriptures and Scripture Insights*. Chicago: Liturgy Training Publications, published annually.

This annual contains the full text of all the readings for Sunday (including the psalm), along with insights about the readings from Scripture scholars, questions for reflection and discussion, and suggestions for action steps.

Daily Prayer. Chicago: Liturgy Training Publications, published annually.

Using a familiar order of prayer (psalm, Scripture, brief reflection, universal prayer, Lord's Prayer, and closing prayer) this annual publication provides prayer for every day of the year. It is ideal for both individuals and groups.

Zimmerman, Joyce Ann, CPPS. *How Deep the Mystery, Meditating on the Words of the Mass*. Chicago: Liturgy Training Publications, 2020.

Even for very attentive participants in the Mass, the words, music, and ritual actions can fly by us so quickly that we don't quite absorb all their meaning. This book, by a noted speaker and writer on the spirituality of the liturgy, presents many of the prayers we hear at Mass, each accompanied by a reflection and questions to ponder.

Glossary

Advent: The liturgical time of joyful preparation and anticipation for Christmas. It is also a time of penance, although this aspect is secondary to the spirit of hope-filled waiting. This time, considered to be the start of a new liturgical year, begins on the fourth Sunday before Christmas.

Ambo: The place from which all the Scripture readings are proclaimed and the homily may be preached during liturgy; a pulpit or lectern. The ambo is also used for singing of the Exsultet, for announcing the intentions of the universal prayer, and for leading the responsorial psalm. The term is derived from a Greek word for "raised place."

Assembly: The people gathered for divine worship; often called the congregation. The *Constitution on the Sacred Liturgy* (no. 7), discussing the many ways Christ is present in the sacrifice of the Mass, says, "He is present . . . when the Church prays and sings, for he promised: 'Where two or three are gathered together in my name, there am I in the midst of them' (Matthew 18:20)." Contemporary liturgical theology emphasizes that it is the assembly as a whole that celebrates the liturgy under the leadership of a priest.

Baptismal Font: The pool or basin where the sacrament of baptism is administered. The font may be located within the main body of the church, either at the entrance, or within the nave in the midst of the assembly, or in the sanctuary, or it may be placed in a separate baptistery.

Blessed Sacrament: The name commonly used to refer to the Eucharistic elements of bread and wine after they have been consecrated and have become the Body and Blood of Christ.

Blessed Sacrament Chapel: A separate chapel in which the tabernacle with the reserved Blessed Sacrament is located.

Book of the Gospels: A ritual book from which the passages from the Gospels prescribed for Masses on Sundays, solemnities, feasts of the Lord and of the saints, and ritual Masses are proclaimed; also called an *evangeliary*. It may be carried in the entrance procession and placed on the altar, and then processed to the ambo during the Gospel acclamation. It is presented to deacons at their ordination and held over the heads of bishops at their ordination.

Catechumen: An unbaptized person who has declared their intention to prepare for the sacraments of initiation and has been accepted into the order of catechumens. Catechumens, though not yet fully initiated, are joined to the Church and are considered part of the household of Christ. The names of those accepted as catechumens are to be written in the register of catechumens kept by the parish.

Christmas Time: The period of the liturgical year beginning with Evening Prayer I of the Nativity of the Lord and ending with Evening Prayer on the Feast of the Baptism of the Lord (which may fall on the Sunday or Monday after Epiphany). This liturgical time commemorates the Incarnation, the birth of Christ, and his first manifestations.

Collect: The opening prayer of the Mass. It sums up or collects the thoughts and prayers of the assembly, and concludes the Introductory Rites. After the collect, everyone is seated and the Liturgy of the Word begins.

Collection: The action of collecting money for the Church and the poor that takes place at Mass after the Universal Prayer. These offerings of money may be brought forward along with the bread and wine in the procession, because they are a sign of the self-offering of the members of the assembly participating in the offering of the sacrifice.

Colors, Liturgical: The official colors of the outer vestments worn by celebrants and assisting deacons. Each day in the liturgical calendar requires a specific color or offers a choice among colors depending upon the liturgical time or the particular Mass being celebrated. By tradition in the Roman Rite, the colors are white, green, red, violet, black, and rose; the determination of which color is used is found in *The Roman Missal* and in the *General Instruction of the Roman Missal*. More precious vestments, usually with gold or silver threads, may be worn on solemn occasions.

Credence Table: The side table on which the vessels and articles needed for the celebration are placed when not in use, particularly during the celebration of the Eucharist.

Dismissal: The final, formal invitation by the deacon or, in his absence, the priest for the assembly to go forth from the liturgical celebration. The word can also refer to the dismissal of the catechumens after the homily at Mass.

Easter: The commemoration of the Resurrection of the Lord, celebrated on the first Sunday after the first full moon after the vernal equinox. The earliest date that Easter can fall is March 22, and the latest is April 25. The celebration of Easter continues for fifty days, a period called Easter Time, and concludes with Evening Prayer on Pentecost Sunday.

Eucharistic Prayer: The central prayer of the Mass. It is an act of thanksgiving, praise, blessing, and consecration. It corresponds to Jesus' act of blessing during the Last Supper.

Extraordinary Minister of Holy Communion: The liturgical minister who is authorized by the bishop to assist priests and deacons in the distribution of holy Communion. An extraordinary minister functions when a sufficient number of ordinary ministers is not present.

Gaudete Sunday: Name given to the Third Sunday of Advent, taken from the first word of the entrance antiphon in Latin, *Gaudete*, "rejoice." Rose-colored vestments may be worn on this day instead of violet.

Gifts: The elements of bread and wine to be consecrated to become the Body and Blood of Christ. The gifts may also be referred to as the offerings.

Gift Table: The table located in the midst of the assembly on which the gifts of bread and wine are placed before they are carried in procession to the altar at the beginning of the Liturgy of the Eucharist.

Hospitality: The practice of being friendly and kind towards guests, of being hospitable, welcoming.

Intercession: One of the specific intentions or prayers that are announced in the universal prayer at Mass or as part of the intercessions in the Liturgy of the Hours.

Laetare Sunday: Name given to the Fourth Sunday of Lent, taken from the first word of the entrance antiphon in Latin, *Rejoice* (from "Rejoice, Jerusalem"). Rose-colored vestments may be worn on this day instead of violet, and flowers may be used to decorate the sanctuary.

Lectionary for Mass: The book containing the Scripture readings proclaimed at Mass, including the responsorial psalms, for each day of the year. The lectionary approved for use in the United States is published in several volumes. The Gospel readings are also contained in a separate *Book of the Gospels*. The *Lectionary for Mass* is not carried in procession but is placed on the ambo before Mass begins so that the readers may read from it.

Lent: The period that precedes the celebration of Christ's passion and resurrection during the Paschal Triduum. Lent is both a time of preparation for baptism and a penitential time; it is approximately forty days long, echoing the forty days of prayer and fasting of Jesus in the desert after his baptism. In the Western Church, it begins on Ash Wednesday and continues for six weeks. It ends prior to the Evening Mass of the Lord's Supper on Holy Thursday. The last week of Lent is called Holy Week. For the elect, Lent is the Period of Purification and Enlightenment, the final preparation for baptism at Easter. For the baptized, Lent is a time for renewal in the meaning and grace of their own baptism.

Liturgy: "The word 'liturgy' originally meant a 'public work' or a 'service in the name of/on behalf of the people.' In Christian tradition it means the participation of the People of God in 'the work of God'" (*Catechism of the Catholic Church*, 1069). Liturgy includes the sacraments, the Liturgy of the Hours, and other rites and rituals, especially the celebration of the Mass.

Narthex: The space inside the entrance of a church where people may gather before or after liturgy. It can be a place of welcome, a transitional space from the outside world into the worship space of the church, and vice versa. Some liturgical moments may occur in the narthex, such as the introductory rites of the Rite of Acceptance into the Order of Catechumens, of the Rite of Baptism for children, and of the Funeral Liturgy.

Nave: The main section of a church building where the assembly gathers for worship. It is the area in the church building for the faithful containing the pews, distinct from the sanctuary.

Offerings: The gifts of bread and wine. They symbolize offering of self that each member of the assembly makes as participation in Christ's offering of himself to God the Father.

Offertory: Term from the Tridentine Missal that sometimes is still used to refer to what is now called the preparation of the gifts. Although the bread and wine are referred to as offerings, this part of the Mass involves their presentation and preparation for the act of offering, which takes place during the Eucharistic Prayer. Nevertheless, the chant that occurs at the preparation of the gifts is still referred to as the offertory chant.

Offertory Procession: Another name used for the procession with the gifts of bread and wine to the altar during Mass—i.e., the presentation of the gifts.

Prayer of the Faithful: Another name for the universal prayer or bidding prayers during the celebration of the Eucharist.

Presider: The title given to the priest celebrant at a celebration of the Eucharist or other liturgy. It differs from the term celebrant in that, while, in a broad sense, everyone in the assembly celebrates the liturgy and the concelebrating priests also celebrate the Mass, only one person in the assembly can preside.

Procession with the Gifts: The bringing forward of the bread and wine by members of the assembly at the beginning of the Liturgy of the Eucharist. Monetary offerings for the Church and for the poor often are brought forward at this time as well. Through this rite the people symbolically present themselves along with the gifts of bread and wine that will be transformed and then received back as the Body and Blood of Christ.

Profound Bow: A bow of the body; a bow from the waist. This type of bow is made to the altar by the ministers in the procession at the beginning and end of Mass and in general whenever anyone in the liturgical assembly passes in front of the altar. Everyone in the liturgical assembly makes a profound bow during the creed, in recognition of the incarnation. There are also prescribed times in the liturgy when the priest and the deacon make profound bows.

Rite of Christian Initiation of Adults (RCIA): The ritual book, part of the Roman Ritual, that gives the norms, directives, and ritual celebrations for initiating unbaptized adults and children who have reached catechetical age into Christ and incorporating them into the church. The RCIA prescribes a sequence of periods, or stages (Evangelization and Precatechumenate, Catechumenate, Purification and Enlightenment, and Postbaptismal Catechesis), and rites by which candidates transition from one stage to another (Acceptance into the Order of Catechumens; Rite of Election), which culminate in the celebration of the sacraments of initiation, usually at the Easter Vigil. The RCIA also includes an adapted process for completing the Christian initiation of baptized but uncatechized Catholics and for bringing baptized but uncatechized non-Catholics into the full communion of the Catholic Church.

Roman Missal: The book or books containing the prayers, hymns, and Scripture readings prescribed for the celebration of Mass. The present-day missal, published in 1970 and currently in its third edition, is subdivided into several books: a book of prayers used by the priest, which is still called the *missal* even though technically the book contains only part of the Roman Missal; the lectionary, which contains the Scripture readings; and the book of hymns and antiphons called the gradual.

Rubric: A direction or explanatory instruction printed between prayers or other spoken texts of a liturgical rites. The word *rubric* is derived from the Latin word for *red* because rubrics are normally printed in red in the liturgical books.

Sacristan: The liturgical minister who has the responsibility for preparing everything needed for liturgical celebrations. The duties of the sacristan include arranging everything needed before the liturgy begins, and cleaning up and putting things away after. Sometimes his or her duties include caring for the sacristy, vestments, vessels, and the good order of the worship space itself.

Sacristy: The room in which vestments and liturgical items are stored and prepared for use before liturgies. It is also commonly used as a vesting room, although larger churches and cathedrals may have a separate vesting room, called the *secretarium*.

Sanctuary: The area of the church in which the presidential chair, altar, and ambo, are located, and in which the primary ministers may also sit. Normally it is somewhat elevated, for the sake of visibility.

Tabernacle: The safe-like receptacle for storing the consecrated Eucharistic bread. When the Blessed Sacrament is present in the tabernacle, it is to be locked and the sanctuary light alight. The tabernacle must be immovable, solid, and not transparent.

Universal Prayer: The intercessory prayers in the celebration of the Mass, following the creed on Sundays and solemnities or the homily on other days; also called the prayer of the faithful or bidding prayers, and formerly called the general intercessions. It consists of an introduction, intentions and responses to the intentions, and a concluding prayer.

Prayer for Ministers of Hospitality

Generous God,

you call each of us to gather,

to give you praise and thanksgiving,

to be fed by your Word and sacrament,

and to love one another.

You sent your Son as a model for hospitality
and ministry.

May I have the courage to walk in his ways
and serve your people.

Open the eyes of my heart to see the gifts
and the needs

of each person who enters your house today.

Give me grace to know my strengths
and weaknesses

and wisdom to respond well

in each situation that may arise.

Grant this through that same Jesus
Christ our Lord.

Amen.